OPPOSING
VIEWPOINTS®
SERIES

Pollution

Other Books of Related Interest:

Opposing Viewpoints Series

Energy Alternatives

At Issue Series

Green Cities

Current Controversies Series

The Green Movement

"Congress shall make
no law . . . abridging
the freedom of speech,
or of the press."

First Amendment to the US Constitution

The basic foundation of our democracy is the First Amendment guarantee of freedom of expression. The *Opposing Viewpoints* series is dedicated to the concept of this basic freedom and the idea that it is more important to practice it than to enshrine it.

OPPOSING VIEWPOINTS® SERIES

I Pollution

Louise I. Gerdes, Book Editor

GREENHAVEN PRESS
A part of Gale, Cengage Learning

GALE
CENGAGE Learning™

Detroit • New York • San Francisco • New Haven, Conn • Waterville, Maine • London

Christine Nasso, *Publisher*
Elizabeth Des Chenes, *Managing Editor*

© 2011 Greenhaven Press, a part of Gale, Cengage Learning.

Gale and Greenhaven Press are registered trademarks used herein under license.

For more information, contact:
Greenhaven Press
27500 Drake Rd.
Farmington Hills, MI 48331-3535
Or you can visit our Internet site at gale.cengage.com

For product information and technology assistance, contact us at

Gale Customer Support, 1-800-877-4253
For permission to use material from this text or product, submit all requests online at www.cengage.com/permissions

Further permissions questions can be emailed to permissionrequest@cengage.com

Articles in Greenhaven Press anthologies are often edited for length to meet page requirements. In addition, original titles of these works are changed to clearly present the main thesis and to explicitly indicate the author's opinion. Every effort is made to ensure that Greenhaven Press accurately reflects the original intent of the authors. Every effort has been made to trace the owners of copyrighted material.

Cover Image copyright © Paul Cooklin/Flicker/Getty Images.

LIBRARY OF CONGRESS CATALOGING-IN-PUBLICATION DATA

Pollution / Louise I. Gerdes, book editor.
    p. cm. -- (Opposing viewpoints)
    Includes bibliographical references and index.
    ISBN 978-0-7377-5231-1 (hardcover) -- ISBN 978-0-7377-5232-8 (pbk.)
    1. Air--Pollution. 2. Air--Pollution--Government policy. I. Gerdes, Louise I., 1953-
    TD883.P582 2011
    363.73--dc22
                                                2010051681

Printed in the United States of America
1 2 3 4 5 6 7 15 14 13 12 11

Contents

Chapter 3: How Can Communities Reduce Pollution?

Chapter 4: What Federal Policies Will Best Reduce Pollution?

Why Consider Opposing Viewpoints?

> "The only way in which a human being can make some approach to knowing the whole of a subject is by hearing what can be said about it by persons of every variety of opinion and studying all modes in which it can be looked at by every character of mind. No wise man ever acquired his wisdom in any mode but this."
>
> *John Stuart Mill*

In our media-intensive culture it is not difficult to find differing opinions. Thousands of newspapers and magazines and dozens of radio and television talk shows resound with differing points of view. The difficulty lies in deciding which opinion to agree with and which "experts" seem the most credible. The more inundated we become with differing opinions and claims, the more essential it is to hone critical reading and thinking skills to evaluate these ideas. Opposing Viewpoints books address this problem directly by presenting stimulating debates that can be used to enhance and teach these skills. The varied opinions contained in each book examine many different aspects of a single issue. While examining these conveniently edited opposing views, readers can develop critical thinking skills such as the ability to compare and contrast authors' credibility, facts, argumentation styles, use of persuasive techniques, and other stylistic tools. In short, the Opposing Viewpoints Series is an ideal way to attain the higher-level thinking and reading skills so essential in a culture of diverse and contradictory opinions.

In addition to providing a tool for critical thinking, *Opposing Viewpoints* books challenge readers to question their own strongly held opinions and assumptions. Most people form their opinions on the basis of upbringing, peer pressure, and personal, cultural, or professional bias. By reading carefully balanced opposing views, readers must directly confront new ideas as well as the opinions of those with whom they disagree. This is not to simplistically argue that everyone who reads opposing views will—or should—change his or her opinion. Instead, the series enhances readers' understanding of their own views by encouraging confrontation with opposing ideas. Careful examination of others' views can lead to the readers' understanding of the logical inconsistencies in their own opinions, perspective on why they hold an opinion, and the consideration of the possibility that their opinion requires further evaluation.

Evaluating Other Opinions

To ensure that this type of examination occurs, *Opposing Viewpoints* books present all types of opinions. Prominent spokespeople on different sides of each issue as well as well-known professionals from many disciplines challenge the reader. An additional goal of the series is to provide a forum for other, less known, or even unpopular viewpoints. The opinion of an ordinary person who has had to make the decision to cut off life support from a terminally ill relative, for example, may be just as valuable and provide just as much insight as a medical ethicist's professional opinion. The editors have two additional purposes in including these less known views. One, the editors encourage readers to respect others' opinions—even when not enhanced by professional credibility. It is only by reading or listening to and objectively evaluating others' ideas that one can determine whether they are worthy of consideration. Two, the inclusion of such viewpoints encourages the important critical thinking skill of objectively evaluating an author's credentials and bias. This evaluation will illuminate an author's reasons for taking a particular stance on an issue and will aid in readers' evaluation of the author's ideas.

It is our hope that these books will give readers a deeper understanding of the issues debated and an appreciation of the complexity of even seemingly simple issues when good and honest people disagree. This awareness is particularly important in a democratic society such as ours in which people enter into public debate to determine the common good. Those with whom one disagrees should not be regarded as enemies but rather as people whose views deserve careful examination and may shed light on one's own.

Thomas Jefferson once said that "difference of opinion leads to inquiry, and inquiry to truth." Jefferson, a broadly educated man, argued that "if a nation expects to be ignorant and free . . . it expects what never was and never will be." As individuals and as a nation, it is imperative that we consider the opinions of others and examine them with skill and discernment. The *Opposing Viewpoints* series is intended to help readers achieve this goal.

David L. Bender and Bruno Leone,
Founders

Introduction

"Most people cannot get those images [of the Deepwater Horizon oil spill] out of their mind, and each time we pump gasoline into our cars we think about it. At this point, the long-term social and cultural impact of this catastrophe has not yet been determined. The political impact will surely follow, but its form is uncertain."

—Steven Cohen,
executive director, Earth Institute,
Columbia University

On April 20, 2010, about fifty miles out in the Gulf of Mexico, a giant burst of methane gas suddenly exploded from the seabed below, shooting the drill pipe of the Deepwater Horizon offshore oil rig to the surface. The gushing gas exploded on the deck of the rig, killing eleven workers. In the months that followed, more than 200 million gallons of oil spilled into the Gulf, polluting coastlines in Louisiana, Mississippi, Alabama, and Florida. In addition to damaging marine and wildlife habitats, the spill was also a serious threat to local economies dependent on fishing and tourism. Shortly after the spill, the call to halt offshore oil drilling gained new momentum. Others countered that the accident should not limit the pursuit of offshore oil, which some consider an important part of the nation's energy strategy. Balancing America's energy needs and the sometimes conflicting need to protect the environment and human health has always been a challenge in the United States. These issues set the background for the debate that followed the Deepwater Horizon disaster and, in many ways, reflect the overarching pollution debate.

That an oil spill should reignite the pollution debate is not surprising. In fact, a massive oil spill off the coast of Santa Barbara, California, in 1969, had a profound influence on public attitudes toward the environment and the energy policies of the time. According to Daniel Yergin, author of the Pulitzer Prize–winning book *The Prize: The Epic Quest for Oil, Money & Power*, "the public outcry, was nationwide and reached right across the political spectrum." Following the 1969 oil spill, the Richard Nixon administration immediately imposed a moratorium on the development of offshore drilling in California. Despite the need for oil at the time, the spill increased opposition to energy development in environmentally sensitive areas, including Alaska, which was seen by many as one of the most promising areas in which to find oil and reduce US dependence on oil from the Middle East.

The Santa Barbara spill also sparked the environmental reform movement of the 1970s. According to Linda Krop, an attorney for the Environmental Defense Center in Santa Barbara, the 1969 spill "had a huge impact, not just on environmental awareness and public response to oil and gas development, but it actually led to almost all of the environmental laws that we know today." Some of the nation's keystone environmental laws were enacted shortly after the Santa Barbara spill. The National Environmental Policy Act of 1970 requires environmental-impact assessment of any federally sanctioned energy projects. The Clean Air Act of 1970 regulated industrial emission, and in the same year Congress created the Environmental Protection Agency (EPA) to enforce environmental laws.

These policies did not, however, prevent other accidents. One of the most memorable in recent history was the oil spill that polluted Alaska's Prince William Sound in 1989. The supertanker *Exxon Valdez* ran aground, and the rupture of the ship's hull released 11 million gallons of oil, killing hundreds of thousands of marine animals and severely damaging the livelihoods of many who lived in the area. Once again, policy makers responded. In 1990 Congress passed the Oil Pollution Act, which created a law allowing placement of legal liability for those responsible for a spill and established a fund to pay for indirect damages. President George H.W. Bush immediately restricted offshore drilling to limited, less vulnerable areas. In 2008, however, President George W. Bush, lifted the ban on drilling in Alaska's Bristol Bay.

After taking office in 2009, President Barack Obama set aside Bush's 2008 offshore drilling policies. As gas prices soared, however, Obama announced in his 2010 State of the Union address that it was necessary to make "tough decisions about opening new offshore areas for oil and gas development." In the *New York Times* on March 31, 2010—three weeks before the Deepwater Horizon spill—Obama proposed opening millions of acres to drilling. He reasoned that "the bottom line is this: given our energy needs, in order to sustain economic growth and produce jobs, and keep our business competitive, we are going to need to harness traditional sources of fuel even as we ramp up production of new sources of renewable, home grown energy." Within three weeks of Obama's statement, the Deepwater Horizon exploded and oil spilled into the Gulf of Mexico. In the months that followed, a debate, much like the one that followed the 1969 Santa Barbara spill, began anew.

In the wake of the public outrage following the Deepwater Horizon oil spill, President Obama called for a moratorium on offshore drilling that was not lifted until six months later. As a result, the conservative Heritage Foundation reported that as many as thirty-six oil rigs were put out of work, leaving twelve thousand without jobs. Nevertheless, according to the *New York Daily News* on June 4, 2010, Obama defended the moratorium, arguing that "until I've got a review that tells me A, what happened; B, how do you prevent a blowout of the sort that we saw; C, even if it's a one-in-a-million chance something like this happens again, that we actually know how to deal with it. . . . Until that happens, it would be irresponsible of me to lift that moratorium." Environmentalists want a permanent ban on new offshore drilling. They claim that the benefits of offshore drilling do not outweigh the risks. "The Deepwater drilling disaster is clear evidence that offshore drilling is a dirty and dangerous business," argues Jacqueline Savitz, pollution campaign director and senior scientist with Oceana, a Washington-based environmental advocacy group. "Any perceived benefits provided by these activities would be equaled, if not exceeded, by their replacement—clean energy—and the risks of offshore drilling are so much greater than any that clean energy could ever create," she argues in a *CQ Researcher* article on June 25, 2010.

Not unlike offshore oil drilling supporters of the past, those who oppose a ban on offshore drilling argue that while the Deepwater Horizon spill was a disaster, bans will merely compound the damage. Indeed, claims H. Sterling Burnett, a scholar at the National Center for Policy Analysis, as a result of the moratorium, "oil-rig workers, suppliers, and employees of associated industries joined Gulf fishermen and hotel employees in the unemployment line." Moreover, supporters suggest that an offshore drilling ban would unnecessarily reduce oil output. As US energy needs grow, they reason, oil will be necessary to promote economic growth and to reduce dependence on foreign oil, especially from hostile regions. Although Burnett agrees that steps must be taken to correct errors that led to the Deepwater Horizon spill, "from the point of view of the economy, national security and environmental quality, halting oil and gas development due to this isolated incident would make a bad situation worse."

These often-conflicting views—that energy policies should reduce the threat of pollution and, alternatively, that energy policies should not interfere with the American pursuit of energy independence—remain one of the fundamental controversies in the pollution debate. This tension is, in fact, reflected in many of the viewpoints presented in the following chapters of *Opposing Viewpoints: Pollution*: How Serious Is the Problem of Pollution? What Technologies Will Best Reduce Pollution? How Can Communities Reduce Pollution? and What Federal Policies Will Best Reduce Pollution? BP, the company that owned the Deepwater Horizon oil rig, effectively capped the oil spill on September 19, 2010. The impact the spill will have on energy and pollution-control policy remains, in the words of journalist Thomas J. Billitteri, "as blurry as the Gulf Coast's polluted waters."

How Serious Is the Problem of Pollution?

Chapter Preface

Whether mercury emitted from coal-fired power plants remains a serious threat to the environment and human health in the United States is one of several controversies in the current pollution debate. Few question that mercury is a dangerous element that poses a serious threat to human health. According to the Environmental Protection Agency (EPA), exposure to any amount greater than 6.3 millionths of one gram of mercury can have serious health consequences. While mercury comes from natural sources such as volcanic eruptions, most of the mercury released into the environment in the United States comes from coal-fired power plants. Mercury emitted into the atmosphere from the burning of coal is then deposited through rain and snow into America's lakes and reservoirs, where it accumulates in the food webs of animals, including fish. Indeed, as of 2006, forty-eight states have issued warnings against eating certain fish species due to mercury contamination from local rivers, lakes, and coastal waters.

The Clean Air Act of 1970 gave the federal government a significant role in reducing air pollution and authorized regulations to limit emissions. The act identifies mercury as a hazardous air pollutant and tasks the EPA with enforcing mercury emission reductions. The EPA agreed in the late 1990s to develop a mercury pollution standard by 2004. Rather than develop stringent limits to reduce mercury emissions, however, the EPA developed a Clean Air Mercury Rule (CAMR) that created a mercury allowance trading program. CAMR creates caps on the total allowable mercury emissions that a state's power plants may release. If plants reduce emissions below their allotment, they can sell their allowances to plants with higher emission rates. When fully implemented in 2025,

EPA officials assert, CAMR will reduce mercury emissions in the United States by 70 percent. This assertion remains hotly contested.

Most energy companies support the new rules. Rather than being forced to install mercury emission control technologies, the rules allow them to choose whether to reduce mercury emissions or buy allowances. According to Michael Rossler of Edison Electric Institute in a 2007 article in *CQ Researcher*, "a national cap-and-trade program is the most cost-effective means to achieve substantial mercury emission reductions." In Rossler's view, energy companies are in the best position to know which strategy will translate into lower electricity costs for consumers. Moreover, energy companies maintain that the most recent technologies for removing mercury emissions need further study before they are accepted as being reliably effective.

CAMR opponents disagree. In fact, they argue, mercury-emission technology has been used with significant success on municipal waste incinerators, which were once a large source of mercury emissions. Moreover, critics of cap-and-trade policies maintain, the new rules will take too long to reduce mercury emissions and will create dangerous concentrations of mercury near sources that buy allowances rather than install pollution-reducing equipment. In 2005, US senators from Vermont and Maine, Patrick J. Leahy and Olympia J. Snow, respectively, proposed a resolution to oppose CAMR. Leahy and Snow represent states in the northeastern United State whose electricity comes primarily from coal-fired power plants. They argued that CAMR "leaves hundreds of plants using antiquated control technology for two or more decades and significantly increases the risk of toxic hotspots downwind of such plants." The resolution was defeated on September 13, 2005, by a narrow margin—47–51. Impacted states continued the fight and since the rule was proposed, sixteen states have filed lawsuits challenging CAMR. As of this writing, the US

Supreme Court has yet to review a Washington, D.C., court decision that ruled in favor of the states and vacated CAMR.

Commentators continue to contest the seriousness of the nation's mercury pollution problem and how to best manage these pollutants while keeping consumer energy costs low. As policy makers explore how best to stimulate America's struggling economy, they also face the often competing challenge of simultaneously protecting human health and the environment. Pollution and waste often accompany growth. The authors in the following chapter debate the seriousness of the pollution threats this growth poses.

| "Unhealthy air remains a threat to the lives and health of millions of people in the United States."

Air Pollution Continues to Be a Serious Problem

American Lung Association

The American Lung Association, which has a mission to improve lung health and prevent lung disease, argues in the following viewpoint that air pollution remains a serious American health threat. While many US cities have shown improvement in particle pollution and ozone levels, the air in others remains polluted, the association asserts. In fact, the association claims, six out of ten people in the United States live in counties with unhealthful air. Those with diabetes, asthma, and chronic lung and cardiovascular disease are particularly vulnerable, the association maintains, especially if they are poor. Policies that strengthen ozone and particle pollution standards and clean up dirty power plants are therefore necessary, the association concludes.

As you read, consider the following questions:

1. In the opinion of the American Lung Association, why does cleaner air show up repeatedly in the monitoring data of *State of the Air 2010*?

American Lung Association, *State of the Air 2010*, pp. 5–9. Reproduced by permission.

2. According to the association, how many people live in the eighteen counties with unhealthful levels of all three pollutants: ozone and short-term and year-round particle pollution?

3. In the association's view, what type of power plant is among the largest contributors to particulate pollution, ozone, mercury, and global warming?

The *State of the Air 2010* shows that air quality in many places has improved, but that over 175 million people— roughly 58 percent—still suffer pollution levels that are too often dangerous to breathe. Unhealthy air remains a threat to the lives and health of millions of people in the United States, despite great progress. Even as the nation explores the complex challenges of global warming and energy, air pollution lingers as a widespread and dangerous reality.

Ranking Methods

The *State of the Air 2010* report looks at levels of ozone and particle pollution found in monitoring sites across the United States in 2006, 2007, and 2008. The report uses the most current quality-assured nationwide data available for these analyses. For particle pollution, the report examines fine particulate matter ($PM_{2.5}$) in two different ways: averaged year-round (annual average) and over short-term levels (24-hour). For both ozone and short-term particle pollution, the analysis used a weighted average number of days that allows recognition of places with higher levels of pollution. For the year-round particle pollution rankings, the report uses averages calculated and reported by the U.S. Environmental Protection Agency [EPA]. For comparison, the *State of the Air 2009* report covered data from 2005, 2006 and 2007.

The strongest improvement came in the year-round (annual) particle pollution levels, but most of the cities with the highest ozone and short-term particle levels improved as well. These results show that cleaning up major sources of air pollution produces healthier air. However, the continuing problem demonstrates that more remains to be done, especially in cleaning up coal-fired power plants and existing diesel engines. The results also show the need for stronger limits on national air pollution levels—a fight that the American Lung Association has long led as a key to healthier air.

For the first time, the *State of the Air 2010* report includes population estimates for another at-risk group, people living in poverty. . . . People who have low incomes face higher risk of harm from air pollution. The population estimates here are based in the poverty definition used by the U.S. Census Bureau.

Evaluating Year-Round Particle Pollution

The *State of the Air 2010* finds great progress in cutting year-round particle pollution, compared to the 2009 report. Thanks to reductions in emissions from coal-fired power plants and the transition to cleaner diesel fuels and engines, cleaner air shows up repeatedly in the monitoring data, especially in the eastern U.S.

Twenty of the 25 metropolitan areas with the worst year-round pollution reported much lower levels of particle pollution in *State of the Air 2010* compared to the 2009 report. Sixteen metropolitan areas reported their lowest levels ever: Pittsburgh-New Castle, PA; Cincinnati-Middletown-Wilmington, OH-KY-IN; St Louis-St. Charles-Farmington, MO-IL; Charleston, WV; Detroit-Warren-Flint, MI; Weirton-Steubenville, WV-OH; Louisville-Jefferson County-Elizabethtown-Scottsburg, KY-IN; Atlanta-Sandy Springs-Gainesville, GA-AL; Huntington-Ashland, WV-KY-OH; Cleveland-Akron-Elyria, OH; Macon-Warner Robins-Fort Valley, GA; Hagerstown-Martinsburg, MD-WV; Knoxville-Sevierville-La Follette, TN; Indianapolis-Anderson-Columbus, IN; Parkersburg-Marietta, WV-OH; and York-Hanover-Gettysburg, PA.

The other cities that improved over the 2009 report were: Birmingham-Hoover-Cullman, AL (which equaled its lowest level ever); Hanford-Corcoran, CA; Houston-Baytown-Huntsville, TX; and Augusta-Richmond County, GA.

A new city moved to the top of the most-polluted by year-round particle levels list. Phoenix-Mesa-Scottsdale, AZ, moved up after new monitoring data in Pinal County reported the highest readings in the nation. Pinal County and Maricopa County comprise the Phoenix-Mesa-Scottsdale, AZ, metropolitan area.

Some cities on this list had higher levels of pollution compared to the 2009 report. Most of the areas with worse year-round levels of particle pollution were in California, with even Los Angeles showing a slightly higher level. Those cities include: Phoenix-Mesa-Scottsdale, AZ; Bakersfield, CA; Los Angeles-Long Beach-Riverside, CA; Visalia-Porterville, CA; Fresno-Madera, CA; and Modesto, CA.

For the first time, six cities on the most-polluted list received passing grades, meaning they met the current, but inadequate, standard for year-round particulate matter, set at 15 micrograms per cubic meter. Those cities are: Hagerstown-Martinsburg, MD-WV; Knoxville-Sevierville-La Follette, TN; Augusta-Richmond County, GA; Indianapolis-Anderson-Columbus, IN; Parkersburg-Marietta, WV-OH; and York-Hanover-Gettysburg, PA. The EPA is reviewing the substantial evidence that the standard is much too lenient and, consequently, fails to provide adequate protection for public health. The [American] Lung Association won a court decision in 2009 requiring EPA to review that evidence. EPA is promising to propose a standard in November 2010.

Rating Short-Term Particle Pollution

Seventeen of the 25 metropolitan areas on this list of the most polluted experienced fewer days of unhealthy levels of particle pollution on average in the *State of the Air 2010* report compared to the 2009 report. Improvements occurred all across the nation. Improving were: Pittsburgh-New Castle, PA; Los Angeles-Long Beach-Riverside, CA; Birmingham-Hoover-Cullman, AL; Sacramento-Arden-Arcade-Yuba City, CA-NV; Salt Lake City-Ogden-Clearfield, UT; Hanford-Corcoran, CA; Merced, CA; Chicago-Naperville-Michigan City, IL-IN-WI; San Diego-Carlsbad-San Marcos, CA; Washington-Baltimore-Northern VA, DC-MD-VA; New York City-Newark-Bridgeport, NY-NJ-CT-PA; Logan, UT-ID; Eugene-Springfield, OR; Harrisburg-Carlisle-Lebanon, PA; San Jose-San Francisco-Oakland, CA; Indianapolis-Anderson-Columbus, IN; and Allentown-Bethlehem-Easton, PA-NJ.

Seven of the most polluted cities reported more days of unhealthy levels on average than in the previous report, while one—Philadelphia-Camden-Vineland, PA-NJ-DE-MD—remained unchanged. The metro areas with worse pollution scores were: Bakersfield, Fresno-Madera, Visalia-Porterville, Modesto, and Stockton—all in California—as well as Provo-Orem, UT, and Phoenix-Mesa-Scottsdale, AZ.

Bakersfield, CA, ranked as the city most polluted by short-term levels of particle pollution, its first time atop this list. Last year's previous number one—Pittsburgh—improved enough to drop to third place.

Looking at Ozone Levels

Fourteen of the 25 most polluted metropolitan areas reported fewer days of unhealthy ozone levels on average in the 2010 report compared to the 2009 report. Ten metropolitan areas had higher averages and one remained unchanged.

Improving were cities across the nation: Sacramento-Arden-Arcade-Yuba City, CA-NV; Houston-Baytown-Huntsville, TX; Charlotte-Gastonia-Salisbury, NC; Phoenix-Mesa-Scottsdale, AZ; Dallas-Fort Worth, TX; El Centro, CA; New York City-Newark-Bridgeport, NY-NJ-CT-PA; Washington-Baltimore-Northern VA, DC-MD-VA; Cincinnati-

Middletown-Wilmington, OH-KY-IN; Atlanta-Sandy Springs-Gainesville, GA-AL; Birmingham-Hoover-Cullman, AL; Las Vegas-Paradise-Pahrump, NV; Philadelphia-Camden-Vineland, PA-NJ-DE-MD; and Baton Rouge-Pierre Part, LA.

All of the cities seeing a higher average number of days were all in California, including Los Angeles-Long Beach-Riverside; Bakersfield; Visalia-Porterville; Fresno-Madera; Hanford-Corcoran; San Diego-Carlsbad-San Marcos; San Luis Obispo-Paso Robles; Merced; Modesto; and Chico.

Los Angeles-Long Beach-Riverside, CA, remains firmly atop the list of cities most polluted by ozone pollution. Los Angeles experienced a slight increase in the weighted average number of days, though still marked its second-best level since the first *State of the Air* reported on ozone levels for 1996 to 1999.

The Cleanest Cities

Fargo-Wahpeton, ND-MN, and Lincoln, NE, emerged as the cleanest cities in the U.S, the only cities to appear on all three lists of cleanest cities. Twelve cities ranked cleanest for both particle pollution measures, though not for ozone: Amarillo, TX; Bangor, ME; Billings, MT; Cape Coral-Ft. Myers, FL; Cheyenne, WY; Ft. Collins-Loveland, CO; Pueblo, CO; Salinas, CA; San Luis Obispo-Paso Robles, CA; Santa Fe-Espanola, NM; Sarasota-Bradenton-Punta Gorda, FL; and Tucson, AZ. Five were among the cleanest cities for ozone and for one of the two particle pollution measures: Bismarck, ND; Brownsville-Harlingen-Raymondville, TX; Duluth, MN-WI; Honolulu, HI; and Port St. Lucie-Sebastian-Vero Beach, FL.

Living with Unhealthful Air

Looking at the nation as a whole, the American Lung Association's *State of the Air 2010* finds—

- *Nearly six of ten people (58%) in the United States live in counties that have unhealthful levels of either ozone or*

EPA Concludes Fine Particle Pollution Poses Serious Health Threats

- Causes early death (both short-term and long-term exposure)
- Causes cardiovascular harm (e.g. heart attacks, strokes, heart disease, congestive heart failure)
- Likely to cause respiratory harm (e.g. worsened asthma, worsened COPD, inflammation)
- May cause cancer
- May cause reproductive and developmental harm

American Lung Association, *State of the Air 2010*.

TAKEN FROM: US Environmental Protection Agency, *Integrated Science Assessment for Particulate Matter*, December 2009. EPA 600/R-08/139F.

particle pollution. Almost 175.3 million Americans live in the 445 counties where they are exposed to unhealthful levels of air pollution in the form of either ozone or short-term or year-round levels of particles.

- *Over half the people in the United States (56%) live in areas with unhealthful levels of ozone.* Counties that were graded F for ozone levels have a combined population of almost 167.3 million. These people live in the 414 counties where the monitored air quality places them at risk for decreased lung function, respiratory infection, lung inflammation and aggravation of respiratory illness. The actual number who breathe unhealthy levels of ozone is likely much larger, since this number does not include people who live in adjacent counties in metropolitan areas where no monitors exist.

- *Nearly one-quarter (23%) of people in the United States live in an area with unhealthful short-term levels of particle pollution.* Nearly 70.4 million Americans live in 94 counties that experienced too many days with unhealthy spikes in particle pollution, a decrease from the last report. Short-term spikes in particle pollution can last from hours to several days and can increase the risk of heart attacks, strokes and emergency room visits for asthma and cardiovascular disease, and most importantly, can increase the risk of early death.

- *Roughly one in ten (9.6%) people in the United States lives in an area with unhealthful year-round levels of particle pollution.* Almost 28.9 million U.S. residents live in areas where chronic levels are regularly a threat to their health. Even when levels are fairly low, exposure to particles over time can increase risk of hospitalization for asthma, damage to the lungs and, significantly, increase the risk of premature death.

- *Roughly one in 13 people—some 23.8 million in the United States—live in 18 counties with unhealthful levels of all three: ozone and short-term and year-round particle pollution.*

People at Greater Risk

With the risks from airborne pollution so great, the American Lung Association seeks to inform people who may be in danger. Many people are at greater risk because of their age or because they have asthma or other chronic lung [diseases], cardiovascular disease or diabetes. Here are the numbers of people in each at-risk group.

- *People with Asthma*—Approximately 3.9 million children and over 10.7 million adults with asthma live in parts of the United States with very high levels of ozone. Nearly 4.6 million adults and nearly 1.7 million children with asthma live in areas with high levels of short-term particle pollution. Nearly 1.8 million adults and over 721,000 children with asthma live in counties with unhealthful levels of year-round particle pollution.

- *Older and Younger*—Over 19.8 million adults age 65 and over and nearly 41.7 million children age 18 and under live in counties with unhealthful ozone levels. Nearly 8.2 million seniors and over 17.6 million children live in counties with unhealthful short-term levels of particle pollution. Over 3.1 million seniors and nearly 7.7 million children live in counties with unhealthful levels of year-round particle pollution.

- *Chronic Bronchitis and Emphysema*—Over 5.4 million people with chronic bronchitis and nearly 2.1 million with emphysema live in counties with unhealthful ozone levels. Nearly 2.3 million people with chronic bronchitis and over 845,000 with emphysema live in counties with unhealthful levels of short-term particle pollution. Nearly 1.0 million people with chronic bronchitis and more than 330,000 with emphysema live in counties with unhealthful year-round levels of particle pollution.

- *Cardiovascular Disease*—Nearly 18.6 million people with cardiovascular diseases live in counties with unhealthful levels of short-term particle pollution; nearly 7.4 million live in counties with unhealthful levels of year-round particle pollution. Cardiovascular diseases include coronary heart disease, heart attacks, strokes, hypertension and angina pectoris.

- *Diabetes*—Nearly 4.5 million people with diabetes live in counties with unhealthful levels of short-term particle pollution; nearly 1.9 million live in counties with unhealthful levels of year-round particle pollution. Research indicates that because diabetics are already at higher risk of cardiovascular disease, they may face increased risk due to the impact of particle pollution on their cardiovascular systems.

- *Poverty*—Over 20.8 million people with incomes meeting the federal poverty definition live in counties with unhealthful levels of ozone. Over 9.8 million people in poverty live in counties with unhealthful levels of short-term particle pollution, and nearly 4.4 million live in counties with unhealthful year-round levels of particle pollution. Evidence shows that people who have low incomes may face higher risk from air pollution.

What Needs to Be Done

Many major challenges require the administration and Congress to take steps to protect the health of the public. Here are a few that the American Lung Association calls for to improve the air we all breathe.

- *Clean up dirty power plants.* Coal-fired power plants are among the largest contributors to particulate pollution, ozone, mercury, and global warming. The EPA should immediately take action to reduce emissions and expand clean-up requirements for power plants nationwide. Congress should also pass the Clean Air Act Amendments of 2010, S. 2995, a bill that will cut life-threatening emissions from power plants.

- *Clean up the existing fleet of dirty diesel vehicles and heavy equipment.* Rules EPA put in effect over the past several years mean that new diesel vehicles and equipment must be much cleaner. Still, the vast majority of diesel trucks, buses and heavy equipment (such as bulldozers) will likely be in use for thousands more miles, spewing dangerous diesel exhaust into communities and neighborhoods. The good news is that affordable technology exists to cut emissions by 90 percent. Congress needs to fund EPA's diesel cleanup ("retrofit") program. Congress should also require that clean diesel equipment should be used in federally funded construction programs.

- *Strengthen the ozone standards.* The [American] Lung Association urges the EPA to adopt a much tighter, more protective national air quality standard for ozone, set at 60 parts per billion. The EPA is currently considering strengthening the standard adopted in March 2008, which they now believe was not strong enough to protect health against the widespread harm from ozone smog. The 2008 decision set 75 ppb [parts per billion] as the standard, despite the unanimous recommendations of EPA's official science advisors that such a level would allow too much ozone to meet the requirements of the Clean Air Act. The American Lung Association challenged the 2008 decision in court, along with several states, public health and environmental groups. In January 2010, the EPA proposed a range for the new standard that met the earlier recommendations of the expert panel and the nation's leading public health organizations. EPA will announce the decision on the new standard in August 2010.

- *Strengthen the particle pollution standards.* In 2006, EPA failed to strengthen the annual standard for fine particles, despite the near unanimous recommendation by their official science advisors. EPA lowered the 24-hour standard, though not to the level the [American] Lung Association recommended. EPA can save thousands of lives each year by dramatically strengthening the annual average and the 24-hour standards. In 2009, the [American] Lung Association challenged that 2006 standard in the U.S. Circuit Court and won. EPA will issue a new proposal for the particle pollution standards in November 2010.

- *Clean up harmful emissions from tailpipes in cars.* EPA needs to set new pollution standards for cars and automobile fuels to reduce nitrogen oxides, hydrocarbons, and particle pollution emissions.

> *"Air pollution has been declining for decades across the United States."*

Air Pollution Is Not a Serious Problem

Joel Schwartz

In the following viewpoint, Joel Schwartz claims that while American energy use and productivity are increasing, air pollution is decreasing. Nevertheless, he maintains, environmental activists have convinced many Americans that air pollution continues to pose a serious threat. This has led to regulations that actually limit and restrict pollution-reduction innovation in an energy industry facing increasing demand, Schwartz maintains. Reasoned analysis, not hyperbole, should govern air quality regulation, he argues. Schwartz, author of No Way Back: Why Air Pollution Will Continue to Decline, *is a fellow at the American Enterprise Institute for Public Policy Research, a libertarian think tank.*

As you read, consider the following questions:

1. According to Schwartz, what EPA efforts will lead to a continued decline in air pollution?

Joel Schwartz, "Blue Skies, High Anxiety," *The American*, May–June 2007. Reproduced by permission.

2. What does the author say is the most serious claim leveled against air pollution?

3. In the author's view, what actions were delivering improved air quality before the EPA was created?

Americans are driving more miles, using more energy, and producing more goods and services than ever. But at the same time, the air quality in America's cities is better than it has been in more than a century—despite the fact that the U.S. population has almost quadrupled and real GDP [gross domestic product] has risen by a factor of nearly thirty.

But Americans aren't aware of this good news—or don't believe it. Polls show the public thinks that air pollution has been steady or even rising over the last few decades, that it will worsen in the future, and that it is still a serious threat to people's health. They are convinced that pollution is a serious problem throughout the country, that it is a major cause of asthma and other respiratory diseases, and that it shortens the lives of tens of thousands of people.

Much of what Americans think they know about air pollution is false. Through exaggeration and sometimes even outright fabrication, the main purveyors of the story—journalists, government regulators, environmentalists, and even health scientists—have created public fear out of all proportion to the actual risks.

Air Pollution Is Declining

Air pollution has been declining for decades across the United States. . . . Between 1980 and 2005, average levels of air pollution fell between 20 percent and 96 percent, depending on the pollutant. For example, sulfur dioxide, which results mainly from the burning of coal and the smelting of some metals, is down 63 percent, while carbon monoxide, the vast majority of which comes from automobiles, is down 74 percent. At the same time, coal usage increased more than 60 percent and miles of driving nearly doubled.

Virtually the entire nation now meets federal standards for sulfur dioxide, carbon monoxide, nitrogen dioxide, and lead. The country is also near full compliance for the U.S. Environmental Protection Agency's [EPA's] older standards for ozone (the "one-hour" standard) and particulate matter (the "PM$_{10}$" standard for airborne particulate matter less than ten micrometers in diameter).

Compliance has also greatly improved for the more stringent ozone and PM [particulate matter] standards the EPA adopted in 1997. In 1980, about 75 percent of the nation's ozone monitors violated the eight-hour ozone standard, but the rate was down to 18 percent at the end of 2005. About 90 percent of the nation violated the fine particulate matter (PM$_{2.5}$, or airborne PM under 2.5 micrometers in diameter) standard in 1980, but the proportion had dropped to 16 percent by the end of 2005.

Air pollution will continue to decline. The EPA tightened automobile emission standards in 1994, 2001, and 2004. The last of those rules requires reductions that will cut automobile emissions (including those from SUVs [sport-utility vehicles] and pickups) by 90 percent below the emissions of the current average car. Even after accounting for expected increases in total miles of driving, the net effect will be a reduction of more than 80 percent in total automobile pollution emissions over the next couple of decades. Emissions from on- and off-road heavy-duty diesel vehicles will follow a similar trajectory as 90 percent reduction requirements come into effect for these vehicles in 2007 and 2010, respectively. Industrial emissions will also continue to fall under the EPA's Clean Air Interstate Rule, which will eliminate most remaining power plant pollution.

Why Americans Are Pessimistic

Despite the nation's spectacular progress, polls show that most Americans think air pollution has stayed the same or even increased, and will worsen in the future. Typical is a 2004 poll by the Foundation for Clean Air Progress, which found that only 29 percent of respondents believed that "America's air quality is better than . . . it was in 1970." Some 38 percent said it was worse, and 31 percent said it was about the same. In fact, by any measurement, air quality is enormously improved.

Nevertheless, it's hardly surprising that Americans are pessimistic about air pollution, since much of the information they receive is at odds with reality. . . .

The lack of context adds to misperceptions about pollution. Clearly, some place in the United States has to be the worst at any given time. But even in the worst areas of the country, air pollution is much lower now than it used to be. Riverside, California, has the highest $PM_{2.5}$ levels in the country, but $PM_{2.5}$ in Riverside has dropped by more than half since the early 1980s, even as the area's population has more than doubled. Ignoring and obscuring these large improvements add to the gap between public perception and actual air quality.

The Myth That Air Pollution Kills

The most serious claim leveled against air pollution is that even at current levels it kills tens of thousands of Americans each year. The EPA credits federal pollution regulation with preventing hundreds of thousands of premature deaths during the last 35 years, and, as a result, believes the Clean Air Act has delivered tens of trillions of dollars in benefits. But the existence of these benefits depends on whether the comparatively low air pollution of the last few decades is deadly. Controlled human and animal studies suggest that it is not.

Even air pollution at levels many times greater than Americans ever breathe doesn't kill laboratory animals. As a recent article in the journal *Regulatory Toxicology and Pharmacology* concluded, "It remains the case that no form of ambient [particulate matter]—other than viruses, bacteria, and biochemical antigens—has been shown, experimentally or clinically, to cause disease or death at concentrations remotely close to U.S. ambient levels."

Researchers cannot, of course, do laboratory studies on people to see if air pollution will kill them. But they can look for milder health effects in human volunteers. Such studies also provide little support for claims of serious harm.

Two major forms of particulate matter—sulfates and nitrates—are simply nontoxic. In fact, ammonium sulfate, the main form of particulate matter from coal-fired power plant emissions, is used as an "inert control"—that is, a substance without any health effects—in human studies of the effects of acidic aerosols. Inhaler medications to reduce airway constriction are delivered in the form of sulfate aerosols. Nevertheless, in a glut of reports with scary titles like "Death, Disease, and Dirty Power" and "Power to Kill," environmentalists have been running an aggressive campaign against coal-fired electricity, claiming that tens of thousands of deaths are caused by power plant particulates.

Even "carbonaceous" particulate matter—the noxious, sooty emissions from diesel trucks and other motor vehicles—causes surprisingly little reaction, at least at concentrations encountered in urban air. Studies sponsored by the Health Effects Institute had healthy and asthmatic volunteers ride an exercise bike while breathing concentrated $PM_{2.5}$ collected in the Los Angeles area, or concentrated diesel exhaust. In both cases, the exposures were many times greater than typical levels in urban air, and even a few times greater than peak levels in the most polluted cities. Nevertheless, there were no changes in symptoms or lung function in either the healthy or asthmatic subjects.

Looking at the Evidence

Controlled laboratory evidence, therefore, indicates that low-level air pollution doesn't cause premature death. The claim that tens of thousands of Americans die each year from even the relatively clean air in modern American cities instead rests on indirect evidence from so-called "observational" epidemiology studies, in which researchers look for correlations between air pollution and risk of death in large groups of people.

Observational studies work with subjects who are not randomly selected and with pollution exposures that are not randomly assigned. Researchers use statistical methods to try to remove the biases inherent in the resulting data. Most epidemiological studies you read about in the newspaper—studies that assess the effects of diet or health habits on the risk of cancer or heart disease, for example—are of this nonrandomized, observational variety.

Most health claims based on such observational studies are turning out to be false when tested in large, randomized clinical trials—a "gold standard" methodology that avoids the biases of observational methods and is the type of study required for drug approvals. Spurious health claims from observational studies have become such a pervasive concern in the medical literature that health researchers have been creating new journals specifically designed to combat the problem.

Perhaps not surprisingly, regulators, environmentalists, and most air pollution epidemiologists have ignored these weaknesses and continue to assume that observational studies provide valid information about air pollution's health effects. They point to the thousands of observational studies that have reported a positive association between low-level air pollution and risk of death as proof that the harm is real. But implementing an invalid methodology over and over again doesn't improve its validity. . . .

Why Is Air Pollution Decreasing?

Still, if air pollution is not the threat most Americans think it is, don't we have the Clean Air Act and aggressive regulatory authorities to thank? Not really.

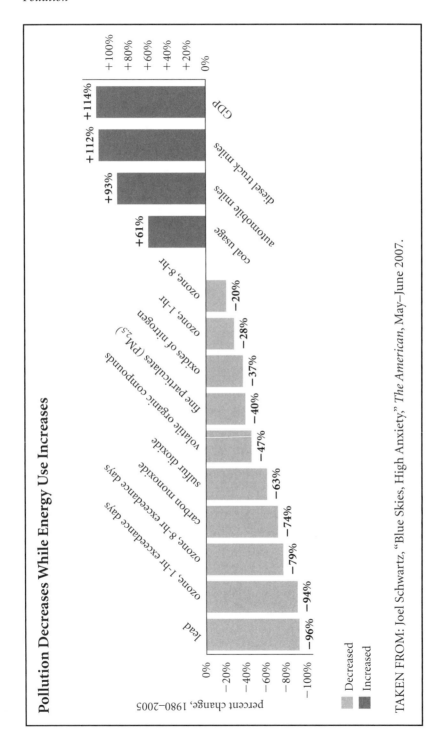

Pollution Decreases While Energy Use Increases

percent change, 1980–2005

GDP +114%

diesel truck miles +112%

automobile miles +93%

coal usage +61%

ozone, 8-hr −20%

ozone, 1-hr −28%

oxides of nitrogen −37%

fine particulates (PM₂.₅) −40%

volatile organic compounds −47%

sulfur dioxide −63%

carbon monoxide −74%

ozone, 8-hr exceedance days −79%

ozone, 1-hr exceedance days −94%

lead −96%

+100%
+80%
+60%
+40%
+20%
0%

0%
−20%
−40%
−60%
−80%
−100%

Decreased
Increased

TAKEN FROM: Joel Schwartz, "Blue Skies, High Anxiety," *The American*, May–June 2007.

Regulators and environmentalists have created the impression that air pollution was on an ever-rising trajectory before the federal government stepped in to protect Americans from unrestrained capitalism. In reality, air pollution had been dropping for decades before the 1970 adoption of the modern Clean Air Act.

Pittsburgh reduced particulate levels by more than 75 percent between the early 1900s and 1970. Chicago, Cincinnati, and New York all have records going back to the 1930s or 1940s showing large reductions in smoke levels. Nationwide monitoring data demonstrate that particulate levels declined nearly 20 percent between 1960 and 1970, while sulfur dioxide declined more than 30 percent. Los Angeles began reducing ozone smog in the 1950s, soon after skyrocketing population and driving created this new form of air pollution. Ozone levels in Los Angeles have been dropping ever since.

Air pollution is not unique in this respect. For decades before the federal government got involved, a range of environmental concerns was being mitigated by a combination of ad hoc local and state regulation, nuisance lawsuits, and market forces that pushed for better efficiency and technology. Other dangers were declining as well. Per mile of driving, the risk of dying in a car accident dropped 75 percent between 1925 and 1966, the year Congress created the National Highway Traffic Safety Administration. The risk of dying on the job declined 55 percent between 1930 and 1971, the inaugural year of the Occupational Safety and Health Administration. And for all of these risks, the rate of improvement was about the same before and after the federal government stepped in.

The Impact of Regulation

After several decades living under what legal scholar David Schoenbrod calls the "modern administrative state," it may seem unimaginable that public goods like cleaner air or safer cars could be delivered without the command and control of powerful national regulators. Unfortunately, we didn't merely trade a decentralized system for an equivalent centralized one. Instead, federal air quality regulation has added a great deal of collateral damage into the bargain.

A good example is a policy called New Source Review (NSR), which requires businesses to install state-of-the-art pollution controls when they build a new plant or upgrade an existing one. Routine repair and maintenance are exempt, allowing existing older plants to keep operating without cleaning up their emissions. The idea was that emissions would decrease over time as existing facilities reached the end of their natural useful lives and were replaced by clean modern plants.

It didn't work out that way. By increasing the costs of new and upgraded plants relative to existing ones, NSR encouraged businesses to keep old plants running as long as possible—ironically slowing progress on air quality. And NSR is just one among many requirements with perverse outcomes.

By the mid- to late-1990s, regulatory economists estimated that the Clean Air Act was costing Americans on the order of 1 to 2 percent of GDP per year—about $1,000 to $2,000 per household. The incremental costs of attaining the tougher ozone and $PM_{2.5}$ standards that the EPA has adopted since then will likely add an additional $1,000 or so a year to the average household's outlay, but will provide little or no incremental health benefit in return.

The EPA's war on pollution marches on, nevertheless. The agency recently adopted a new $PM_{2.5}$ standard, and plans to propose a tougher ozone standard in June [2007] that will represent a vast expansion of the Clean Air Act's reach. About 23 percent of the nation's metropolitan areas violate the current standard. This fraction would double even under the EPA's least stringent alternative. Under the most stringent alternative, literally the entire nation would become a Clean Air Act "non-attainment" area.

Conflicts of Interest

Federal air quality regulation suffers from incentives to create requirements that are unnecessarily stringent, intrusive, bureaucratic, and costly. The Clean Air Act charges the EPA with setting air pollution health standards. But this means that federal regulators decide when their own jobs are finished. Not surprisingly, no matter how clean the air, the EPA continues to find unacceptable risks. The EPA is like a company that gets to decide how much of its product customers must buy. Congress also charges the agency with evaluating the costs and benefits of its own programs. Not surprisingly, the EPA finds the benefits to be far in excess of the costs.

But the conflicts of interest go much deeper. The EPA and state regulators' powers and budgets depend on a continued public perception that there is a serious problem to solve, yet regulators are also major funders of the health research intended to demonstrate the need for more regulation. Regulators decide what questions are asked, which scientists are funded to answer them, and how the results are portrayed. Regulators also provide millions of dollars a year to environmental groups, which use the money to augment fear of pollution and seek increases in regulators' powers.

Before the EPA was created, decentralized actions were delivering the improved air quality that an increasingly wealthy and educated polity was demanding. Before the era of compulsively detailed regulation, the government's role was, to paraphrase economist Sam Peltzman, complementary to market forces, evolving gradually and incrementally, and largely working in concert with people's values and preferences.

By contrast, today's federal regulatory system imposes revolutionary institutional changes that often override people's preferences and suppress individual initiative and creativity. Schoenbrod, a law professor and a senior fellow at the Cato Institute, began his career as an idealistic attorney for the Natural Resources Defense Council during the 1970s. But his experiences convinced him that the modern administrative state is unkind to the people it claims to be protecting. Regulators, he says, have "left the public more anxious about pollution than ever. Such anxiety fuels the growing power of the administrative state."

Improving Regulation

The prospects for improving air quality regulation are not encouraging. Even the [George W.] Bush administration has aided alarmism rather than reform. Environmentalists and many newspaper editorial boards have relentlessly pilloried the president for supposedly "gutting" the Clean Air Act and increasing air pollution. Meanwhile, back in the real world, air pollution continues to hit new record lows; the Bush EPA has imposed the nation's toughest-ever air pollution standards and regulations, going far beyond where the [Bill] Clinton administration chose to tread; and, perhaps most ironic, the Bush administration has justified this vast expansion of the Clean Air Act based on the same spurious health claims through which environmentalists and regulators maintain unwarranted public anxiety.

Realistic public information on air quality is a prerequisite for popular support for a sensible regulatory system focused on results and net improvements in Americans' welfare. Unfortunately, the media have so far shown little interest in improving environmental reporting. True, many journalists realize that environmentalists are often prone to exaggeration and that the regulatory system suffers from significant structural problems. But they also seem to believe regulators and environmentalists are well intentioned, while the critics of regulation must have nefarious motives. Alas, speculation about motives is a poor basis for judging the value of public policies or regulatory institutions. As C.S. Lewis wrote, "Of all tyrannies, a tyranny sincerely exercised for the good of its victims may be the most oppressive. ... [T]hose who torment us for our own good will torment us without end for they do so with the approval of their own conscience."

> "E-waste contains a witch's brew of toxic materials, ranging from heavy metals such as lead, lithium, and cadmium to brominated flame retardants and carcinogens such as beryllium."

Electronic Waste Is a Serious Problem

Kurt Marko

Kurt Marko asserts in the following viewpoint that while municipal waste is declining, electronic waste—cell phones, TVs, monitors, computers, and their peripherals—is increasing. Moreover, he claims, unlike bottles and cans, e-waste can be extremely toxic. Unfortunately, Marko maintains, despite government and private efforts to safely recycle e-waste, unscrupulous scrap dealers are diverting e-waste to developing nations where workers extract precious metals and salvageable components under unsafe conditions. Thus, he reasons, broader efforts to recycle and safely dispose of electronics over their full life cycle are necessary. Marko writes on information technology issues for Processor *magazine.*

As you read, consider the following questions:

1. In Marko's opinion, how does the recycling of e-waste in 2007 compare to the recycling of major appliances?

2. According to the author, how do workers in China, India, Vietnam, and Pakistan handle the e-waste exported there?

3. What does the author claim is phase two of the EPA's four-phase framework for modeling the electronic equipment life cycle?

Recycling is one of those concepts everyone embraces. Yet, when it comes to electronics—TVs, monitors, computers, and peripherals—why do so few of us actually do it? According to figures from the U.S. EPA (Environmental Protection Agency), only about 13.6% of so-called e-waste was recycled in 2007, the rest being diverted to municipal landfills or storage. The rate is a significant improvement from the 10% recycled in 2000; however, it's a far cry from the two-thirds of major appliances—things such as refrigerators and washing machines—that are diverted from the dump.

Clogging Landfills

Thanks to local recycling programs, the overall volume of municipal waste is actually declining year to year; however, the amount of e-waste clogging landfills is increasing 8% annually. Recycling of IT [information technology] consumables is even rarer. According to Brian Musil, senior storage acquisitions manager at RecycleYourMedia.com, a recent study found that only 3% of backup tapes are recycled, leaving about 10 million pounds a year of plastics and assorted metallic coatings in the trash.

Low recycling rates are compounded by our unrelenting consumption of a growing array of electronic devices. According to IDC [International Data Corporation, an IT market intelligence company] estimates, more than 71 million computers were sold in the United States last year [2008], with the worldwide total topping 300 million and expected to hit 425 million in 2012. That's generating a lot of high-tech garbage—material much more toxic than the bottles and cans homeowners toss in their recycling bins.

The Problems with Disposal

E-waste taken to a recycler sometimes ends up in a landfill, just not in this country. Some purported recycling firms are nothing more than collectors of high-tech garbage, using the cover of recycling to generate business and collect fees but then shipping the material to an overseas landfill.

According to the Electronics TakeBack Coalition, "a large portion of the hazardous electronic waste collected for recycling in the U.S. is actually exported to developing countries. There the products are dismantled and separated using such crude and toxic technologies that workers and communities are exposed to many highly toxic chemicals." They point out that, "In countries like China, India, Vietnam, and Pakistan, workers in e-waste yards (working with few health and safety protections) actually 'recycle' very little of these products—they use hammers, acids, and open burning to reclaim some of the materials and burn the rest." A November *60 Minutes* feature by Scott Pelley graphically documented how waste collected in the United States ends up smuggled via an arguably illegal underground sewer to the Far East, where it's broken down for the precious metals and other salvageable components inside.

Regulating Responsible Recycling

Some states, most notably California, have addressed the problem of unscrupulous scrap dealers by instituting fees on certain electronics products to fund programs that evaluate and register prospective recyclers. The EPA has proposed a similar

A Rushing Stream of Electronics

Over the past two decades or more, rapid technological advances have doubled the computing capacity of semiconductor chips almost every eighteen months, bringing us faster computers, smaller cell phones, more efficient machinery and appliances, and an increasing demand for new products. Yet this rushing stream of amazing electronics leaves in its wake environmental degradation and a large volume of hazardous waste—waste created in the collection of the raw materials that go into these products, by the manufacturing process, and by the disposal of these products at the end of their remarkably short lives.

Elizabeth Grossman,
"Chapter 1: The Underside of High Tech," High Tech Trash:
Digital Devices, Hidden Toxics, and Human Health.
Washington, DC: Island Press, 2006.

certification standard, the R2 (Responsible Recycling) Practices, that outlines general principles and specific practices for recyclers disassembling or reclaiming used electronics equipment; however, unlike California's program, R2 is purely voluntary and lacks the force of law.

The environmental activist group Basel Action Network claims that the R2 standards are anything but responsible when it comes to toxic materials. They contend that the standard does little to address the biggest problems in the electronics recycling industry: export of toxic e-waste to developing nations, the landfilling or incineration of e-waste domestically, and the regulation of health and safety conditions for recycling workers, particularly those in prison-based operations.

Given the lax state of recycler regulation, it can be difficult to find a reputable organization. However, organizations such as the Electronics TakeBack Coalition maintain online listings of firms who have signed their responsible recycler pledge (tinyurl.com/98ajce). In addition, Musil notes that firms specializing in media reuse, such as RecycleYourMedia.com (www.recycleyourmedia.com) or NSA [National Sales Associates] (www.nsainc.net), typically perform the due diligence on their recycling partners to ensure unusable material is properly recycled.

An Electronic Equipment Life Cycle Framework

While users often focus on recycling and salvage, this is actually the tail end of the product life cycle. Many products can be resold or reused several times before ending up in the scrap heap. The EPA has developed a four-phase framework for modeling the electronic equipment life cycle. After a product is no longer useful to the original purchaser, phase two is to find it another productive home, via resale or donation to a nonprofit. Recycling comes at phase three of the life cycle, once a product has run its course with the secondary owner; however, even at this stage, a recycling organization may be able to resell the item to a tertiary user, typically in a developing country.

PR [public relations] agency Citigate Cunningham offers a textbook implementation of the EPA's life cycle framework. CEO Christine Pfendt says that her firm has a four-tier process for disposing of old equipment. Its first option is to resell newer equipment, typically by posting an ad on Craigslist. Usable hardware with little resale value, most notably cell phones, is donated to a nonprofit. While Citigate usually does not use equipment brokers, it has sold some items through an online marketplace. Items that are obsolete or broken are taken to local recyclers the firm has vetted.

Pfendt says that the process is easy to manage, with the hardest aspect being asset identification and reconciliation—it's important to ensure that old equipment is purged from their financial records. Enterprises concerned about the administrative overhead of managing a reuse and recycling program can turn to one of the many used equipment brokers, such as CCNY [Computer Connection of Central New York] (www.ccny.com) or DMD Systems Recovery (www.dmdsystems .com), that provide a convenient turnkey solution.

E-waste contains a witch's brew of toxic materials, ranging from heavy metals such as lead, lithium, and cadmium to brominated flame retardants and carcinogens such as beryllium. The increasing production of electronic components is causing a concomitant increase in the e-waste stream, while the low rates of reuse and recycling pose a problem for both domestic and foreign landfills. Yet going green by adopting a reuse and recycling policy for computer equipment and consumables needs not be burdensome and can provide a small financial return on resold hardware or media.

> *"If producers have to deal with their own product waste they will have more incentive to use recyclable materials or materials that will not generate hazardous waste management costs for them."*

Producer Responsibility Can Limit the Impact of Electronic Waste

Beverly Thorpe

In the following viewpoint, Beverly Thorpe argues that making the companies that produce electronic products responsible for their products' entire life cycle will limit the impact of electronic waste. Producer responsibility motivates companies to create products that use recyclable materials and do not generate hazardous waste, she asserts. Moreover, Thorpe maintains, individual producer responsibility encourages eco-design more than collective industry responsibility, which diffuses responsibility and therefore provides no incentive to improve product design. Indeed, Thorpe asserts, more companies now realize that im-

Beverly Thorpe, "How Producer Responsibility for Product Take-Back Can Promote Eco-Design," Cleanproduction.org, March 2008. Reproduced by permission.

proved product design can increase their financial advantage. Thorpe is the communications director of Clean Production Action, an organization that promotes clean production strategies.

As you read, consider the following questions:

1. What does Thorpe say distinguishes extended producer responsibility from a mere take-back system?

2. In the author's view, what is the problem with a flat fee for recycling?

3. According to the author, what is the most common form of brand-specific take-back?

Extended Producer Responsibility (EPR) often termed producer take-back, is an increasingly popular waste policy that is radically different from traditional recycling practices. This is because EPR makes the producer of the product responsible for the financial and/or physical responsibility for product recycling. In its true form EPR also extends the responsibility of the producer to the entire life cycle of the product chain—from production through to end-of-life waste management. However, the end-of-life product stage has become the popular focus for most EPR policy and in Europe producers are now financially responsible for the take-back and recycling of batteries, packaging, vehicles and all electrical and electronic consumer products. In Japan producers are responsible for recycling cars and electronic products and in Canada many provinces are now passing take-back laws for paints, batteries, tires, packaging and electronics. Almost half the states in the US have passed or are about to pass take-back legislation for electronic waste.

Promoting Eco-Design

In an effective EPR scheme the true cost of waste management is internalized within the retail price and companies, because they are now financially responsible, will seek to reduce these costs to remain competitive. This in turn promotes eco-design of products because it is assumed that if producers have to deal with their own product waste they will have more incentive to use recyclable materials or materials that will not generate hazardous waste management costs for them. The establishment of these feedback loops from the downstream (waste handling) to the upstream (the producer of the product) is the core of EPR that distinguishes EPR from a mere take-back system. For example it becomes cost effective for a product designer not to use a mercury switch in an electronic appliance if this will result in not paying hazardous waste costs at the product's end-of-life stage. Instead the designer would more likely substitute a non-mercury alternative, even if it costs slightly more. Also producers would design for re-use, and case of disassembly and recycling because this would also save them money.

The goal of eco-design is stated in the preamble of producer responsibility legislation for cars and electronic products in Europe and the Environment Commissioner at the time the Waste from Electrical and Electronic Equipment (WEEE) Directive was implemented, announced:

> *"I am particularly pleased we could convince Member States to strengthen the individual responsibility of producers for the waste from their product. This will be an important incentive for producers to take environmental consequences into account already when they stand around the design table."*

The Incentives for Eco-Design

In reality the link between eco-design and producer responsibility is complex and evolving. It is therefore essential that all EPR frameworks ensure that producers can achieve credit for eco-design changes in their products. The following summarizes some of the lessons learned to date.

- *A take-back system based on Individual Producer Responsibility (IPR) ensures that producers are responsible for recycling their own products*

Individual producer responsibility (IPR) is a policy tool that makes producers financially and/or physically responsible for the end-of-life management of their own products. This is different from collective responsibility where the industry sector as a whole is responsible for the financial cost of collecting and recycling all products, regardless of brand-name differentiation. IPR ensures that producers are responsible for recycling their own products and this has been implemented in various ways.

In Europe, for example, the WEEE Directive promotes IPR for new electronic products put on the market as of 13 August 2005. For older historical e-waste and for orphan products, whose producers are no longer on the market, producers in the EU are collectively responsible and pay a portion of the total costs of collection and recycling according to their current market share. It was argued that because historical waste such as old TVs were often made with hazardous and unrecyclable materials, they can not be redesigned retroactively, which is why a time-limited period for a collective responsibility approach to historic waste was allowed. However, Europeans envisage that once this historical and orphan waste is cleaned up—for instance by 2020—true individual producer responsibility can be realized which is the main goal of the legislation.

In the US many states have observed that European nation-states may not adequately transpose the WEEE Directive to ensure this transition to full IPR and have therefore taken the proactive step of implementing an all encompassing IPR system from the start. When an IPR-only system is used for both historic and future waste, an additional mechanism needs to be included to pay for orphan products. In the US, this is accomplished by dividing orphan waste costs among the existing companies—sometimes by market share, sometimes by return share.

The Problem with Flat Fees

- *A flat fee on products, regardless of brand, gives no credit for eco-design initiatives.*

Many legislators in the US and Canada recommend a fee on new products to finance the cost of recycling both historic and future waste. However, the standardization of fees on all products, regardless of the brand, provides no direct feedback to the producer for eco-design changes in new products. The system may seem to guarantee funding for recycling into the future but making producers individually responsible for new products is more competitive and allows companies to achieve credit for eco-design changes through market instruments.

For example, producers in Europe are currently allowed to charge a visible fee on new products to pay for the recycling costs of historic waste and orphan waste. This fee is only allowed for a fixed period (8–10 years depending on product category) after which producers will have to incorporate the waste management costs into the retail price of their products. This is very different from the California system—the only US state to use a visible fee—where the fee is collected not by the manufacturers but by the state government who pays for recycling. The manufacturers are not in the loop at all nor is there a plan to transition to IPR for future waste.

In addition producers are also required in Europe to provide a financial guarantee to prevent the costs of future orphan products from falling on society or the remaining producers if a producer goes bankrupt. In Sweden, for example, car producers pay a guarantee to an insurance company which negotiates different premiums with each producer. Estimated future recycling costs are based on test scrapping and the easier the car is to recycle, the lower the premium.

The Benefits of a Large-Scale Take-Back System

- *Differentiating brand-name products can be done in a large-scale take-back system.*

It is often assumed that individual producer responsibility would entail each producer setting up their own take-back and recycling system. This is not the case. A producer could set up their own brand specific take-back system or they can join a collective system in which their brands can be identified.

The most common form of brand-specific take-back is the business-to-business (B2B) models where take-back is often bundled with other value-added services such as data removal and installation services of new equipment. Since 1991 Xerox Corporation's business leasing model, for example, has enabled it to build up a comprehensive design for environment program whereby products are repaired or remanufactured.

In a collective scheme producers can separate out their products in a variety of ways to pay the true cost of their product take-back and recycling. Indeed, this is happening in some collective schemes operating today.

Products can be sorted by brand once they are collected from consumers at collection points such as retailers and municipal collection points. For instance in Switzerland coffee machines are separated out from the rest of WEEE by retailers and then producers pay for their recycling at their own facilities. In Sweden and Norway computers and other IT [information technology] equipment are sorted at the separate collection points by an intermediary company upon request and the cost of recovery is paid for by cost internalization. In Japan retailers, municipalities and others bring discarded large home appliances, such as stoves and refrigerators, to two regional stations depending on the brands. The appliances are then recovered in the company's own facility or the producers contract with other producers and recyclers.

Brand-name differentiation can also be done at the recovery facilities themselves. In Japan each large home appliance has a manifest attached to each product which distinguishes the brand name and the model of the respective producers. In

Switzerland periodic sampling of IT equipment takes place to determine the average amount of products taken back of a particular brand. The producers then pay for their return share in the total waste stream. In the United States, both Maine and Washington states have advocated IPR for e-waste through return share.

Public Support from Many Companies

- *The transition to full Individual Producer Responsibility is supported by many companies.*

In a collective system where producers are jointly responsible for the recycling of all products, including the products sold in the future, there is no incentive to design products to be easier to recycle. That is because producers would simply be paying a proportion of the total cost based on their market share. This may be a temporary option for historic waste, as discussed above, but it provides no incentive for cost-effective eco-design changes in new products. As business proponents of IPR point out, collective producer responsibility may in fact achieve the opposite since "the costs of recycling will be the same for a product that has been designed to be easier to recycle and a product that is much more difficult to disassemble and recycle."

Costs to producers based on return share where discarded products are separated by brand or by random sampling at recycling facilities is a better reflection of the true cost to recycle their products and even provides an incentive to design for durability. It is anticipated that product identification at recycling sites using radio frequency identification (RFID) will be mainstream in the near future and this could also provide recyclers with material and treatment information. . . .

There are a number of producers that now publicly support IPR. Dell's Global Recycling Policy officially supports IPR and offers free take-back of computer systems of any brand when purchasing a new Dell system as well as free take-back of its own brand worldwide. Apple offers free recycling with purchase and Sony offers free take-back of its products in North America. HP [Hewlett-Packard] is also a strong promoter of IPR and is working to ensure global coverage.

Other companies now publicly support IPR including Samsung, Sony Ericsson, Lenovo, LGE, Fujitsu-Siemens, Nokia, and Acer. Electrolux is a champion of IPR and along with Sony, Braun and HP established the European Recycling Platform in 2003 to advocate for IPR. Other companies and NGOs [nongovernmental organizations] have formed a group to lobby for proper implementation of individual producer responsibility in take-back legislation as well as research eco-design incentives. As one member asks: "The question producers should ask themselves in developing their approach to EPR is perhaps not *'how do we implement individual responsibility for our branded products,'* but *'how do we secure financial advantage from our improved designs.'"*

Proactive Product Design

- *Anticipating Individual Producer Responsibility Legislation has led to proactive product design change.*

Interviews with Japanese electronic manufacturers and Swedish car manufacturers in 2000 reveal that the anticipation of EPR regulations, which companies anticipated would make them individually (not collectively) financially responsible for their end-of-life products, was a catalyst for redesigning products to be more recyclable and less toxic. While European take-back directives were being drafted, Japan was also developing its own take-back laws. EPR legislation sent signals to producers that end-of-life costs would have to be factored into future product design.

In particular the European directives on End of Life Vehicles, Waste from Electrical and Electronic Equipment, and the Restriction on Hazardous Substances (RoHS) catalyzed the Japanese industry to be proactive and ahead of their European competitors. In response to growing EPR legislation initiatives companies took a variety of financial and resource-saving measures. NEC, Hitachi, Fujitsu, Matsushita and Sony replaced plastic housings with magnesium alloy—a more recyclable material—for TV cabinets and personal computers. Similarly Matsushita, Sharp, Mitsubishi, Ricoh, and Hitachi switched to more standardized types and grades of plastics for their products. Hitachi and Mitsubishi focused on easier repair and maintenance of their products while NEC, Ricoh and Fujitsu adopted modular designs to facilitate component reuse. The impending RoHS directive provided the incentive for Japanese manufacturers to be ahead of European law by switching to lead-free solders.

Car manufacturers in Sweden and Japan also reacted to impending EPR legislation through design change. Swedish car manufacturers, in particular Volvo, SAAB, and Volvo Trucks established lists of substances targeted for phaseout and worked on improving vehicle design for quicker disassembly and better recycling. Toyota succeeded in developing thermoplastics called TSOP (Toyota Super Olefin Polymer) that can be recycled for the same purpose (recycling instead of down cycling), while having other properties such as durability and mould-ability. It also started to use polyurethane and fibers recovered from auto-shredder dust as noise buffers in new cars. Fuji Heavy Industry established a system of collecting glass from end-of-life vehicles and recycling it for glass wool.

> "Every single molecule of plastic that has ever been manufactured is still somewhere in the environment, and some 100 million tons of it are floating in the oceans."

Plastic Debris Is Polluting the World's Oceans

Richard Grant

Richard Grant reports in the following viewpoint that a patch of garbage made mostly of plastic has accumulated in the Pacific Ocean in an area where major sea currents converge. Those studying the garbage patch argue that the surrounding water contains six times more plastic than plankton, he explains. Unfortunately, Grant affirms, plastic kills marine mammals, birds, and turtles. Moreover, he asserts, because plastic does not biodegrade, those who are concerned about its impact are not quite sure what, if anything, can be done. Nevertheless, he claims, scientists and activists continue to study the patch, looking for answers. Grant, a British writer living in Tucson, Arizona, regularly writes for the Telegraph, *a British newspaper.*

As you read, consider the following questions:

1. According to Grant, what is the basic raw material used to manufacture all the plastic items in our lives?

2. How long does the author claim the marine plastic debris that ends up on the ocean floor will remain there?

3. What, according to the author, is the point of David de Rothschild's voyage on the *Plastiki*?

Way out in the Pacific Ocean, in an area once known as the doldrums, an enormous, accidental monument to modern society has formed. Invisible to satellites, poorly understood by scientists and perhaps twice the size of France, the Great Pacific Garbage Patch is not a solid mass, as is sometimes imagined, but a kind of marine soup whose main ingredient is floating plastic debris.

It was discovered in 1997 by a Californian sailor, surfer, volunteer environmentalist and early-retired furniture restorer named Charles Moore, who was heading home with his crew from a sailing race in Hawaii, at the helm of a 50ft [foot] catamaran that he had built himself.

A Disheartening Discovery

For the hell of it, he decided to turn on the engine and take a shortcut across the edge of the North Pacific Subtropical Gyre, a region that seafarers have long avoided. It is a perennial high-pressure zone, an immense slowly spiralling vortex of warm equatorial air that pulls in winds and turns them gently until they expire. Several major sea currents also converge in the gyre and bring with them most of the flotsam from the Pacific coasts of Southeast Asia, North America, Canada and Mexico. Fifty years ago nearly all that flotsam was biodegradable. These days it is 90 percent plastic.

'It took us a week to get across and there was always some plastic thing bobbing by,' says Moore, who speaks in a jaded, sardonic drawl that occasionally flares up into heartfelt oratory. 'Bottle caps, toothbrushes, Styrofoam cups, detergent bottles, pieces of polystyrene packaging and plastic bags. Half of it was just little chips that we couldn't identify. It wasn't a revelation so much as a gradual sinking feeling that something was terribly wrong here. Two years later I went back with a fine-mesh net, and that was the real mind-boggling discovery.'

Floating beneath the surface of the water, to a depth of 10 metres, was a multitude of small plastic flecks and particles, in many colours, swirling like snowflakes or fish food. An awful thought occurred to Moore and he started measuring the weight of plastic in the water compared to that of plankton. Plastic won, and it wasn't even close. 'We found six times more plastic than plankton, and this was just colossal,' he says. 'No one had any idea this was happening, or what it might mean for marine ecosystems, or even where all this stuff was coming from.'

Exploring the Great Pacific Garbage Patch

So ended Moore's retirement. He turned his small volunteer environmental monitoring group into the Algalita Marine Research Foundation, enlisted scientists, launched public awareness campaigns and devoted all his considerable energies to exploring what would become known as the Great Pacific Garbage Patch and studying the broader problem of marine plastic pollution, which is accumulating in all the world's oceans.

The world's navies and commercial shipping fleets make a significant contribution, he discovered, throwing some 639,000 plastic containers overboard every day, along with their other litter. But after a few more years of sampling ocean water in the gyre and near the mouths of Los Angeles streams, and comparing notes with scientists in Japan and Britain, Moore concluded that 80 percent of marine plastic was initially discarded on land, and the United Nations Environment Programme agrees.

The wind blows plastic rubbish out of littered streets and landfills, and lorries and trains on their way to landfills. It gets into rivers, streams and storm drains and then rides the tides and currents out to sea. Litter dropped by people at the beach is also a major source.

Plastic does not biodegrade; no microbe has yet evolved that can feed on it. But it does photodegrade. Prolonged exposure to sunlight causes polymer chains to break down into smaller and smaller pieces, a process accelerated by physical friction, such as being blown across a beach or rolled by waves. This accounts for most of the flecks and fragments in the enormous plastic soup at the becalmed heart of the Pacific, but Moore also found a fantastic profusion of uniformly shaped pellets about 2mm [millimetres] across.

An Abundance of Mermaids' Tears

Nearly all the plastic items in our lives begin as these little manufactured pellets of raw plastic resin, which are known in the industry as nurdles. More than 100 billion kilograms of them are shipped around the world every year, delivered to processing plants and then heated up, treated with other chemicals, stretched and moulded into our familiar products, containers and packaging.

During their loadings and unloadings, however, nurdles have a knack for spilling and escaping. They are light enough to become airborne in a good wind. They float wonderfully and can now be found in every ocean in the world, hence their new nickname: mermaids' tears. You can find nurdles in abundance on almost any seashore in Britain, where litter has increased by 90 percent in the past 10 years, or on the remotest uninhabited Pacific islands, along with all kinds of other plastic confetti.

'There's no such thing as a pristine sandy beach any more,' Charles Moore says. 'The ones that look pristine are usually groomed, and if you look closely you can always find plastic particles. On Kamilo Beach in Hawaii there are now more plastic particles than sand particles until you dig a foot down. On Pagan Island [between Hawaii and the Philippines] they have what they call the "shopping beach". If the islanders need a cigarette lighter, or some flip-flops, or a toy, or a ball for their kids, they go down to the shopping beach and pick it out of all the plastic trash that's washed up there from thousands of miles away.'

On Midway Island, 2,800 miles west of California and 2,200 miles east of Japan, the British wildlife filmmaker Rebecca Hosking found that many thousands of Laysan albatross chicks are dying every year from eating pieces of plastic that their parents mistake for food and bring back for them.

The Impact on Wildlife

Worldwide, according to the United Nations Environment Programme, plastic is killing a million seabirds a year, and 100,000 marine mammals and turtles. It kills by entanglement, most commonly in discarded synthetic fishing lines and nets. It kills by choking throats and gullets and clogging up digestive tracts, leading to fatal constipation. Bottle caps, pocket combs, cigarette lighters, tampon applicators, cotton bud shafts, toothbrushes, toys, syringes and plastic shopping bags are routinely found in the stomachs of dead seabirds and turtles.

A study of fulmar carcases that washed up on North Sea coastlines found that 95 per cent had plastic in their stomachs—an average of 45 pieces per bird.

Plastic particles are not thought to be toxic themselves but they attract and accumulate chemical poisons already in the water such as DDT and PCBs[1]—nurdles have a special knack

1. DDT, an insecticide that is also toxic to animals and humans, has been banned in the United States since 1972. Developed in the 1930s and banned from production in the 1970s, PCBs are organic compounds used in the manufacture of plastics and as a coolant in electric transformers. PCBs were discovered to be highly toxic to aquatic life and are still found in the environment because they persist for long periods and are biologically accumulative.

for this. Plastic has been found inside zooplankton and filter feeders such as mussels and barnacles; the worry is that these plastic pellets and associated toxins are travelling through the marine food chains into the fish on our plates. Scientists don't know because they are only just beginning to study it.

We do know that whales are ingesting plenty of plastic along with their plankton, and that whales have high concentrations of DDT, PCBs and mercury in their flesh, but that's not proof. The whales could be getting their toxins directly from the water or by other vectors.

Research on marine plastic debris is still in its infancy and woefully underfunded, but we know that there are six major subtropical gyres in the world's oceans—their combined area amounts to a quarter of the earth's surface—and that they are all accumulating plastic soup.

The Great Pacific Garbage Patch has now been tentatively mapped into an east and west section and the combined weight of plastic there is estimated at three million tons and increasing steadily. It appears to be the big daddy of them all, but we do not know for sure.

Dr Pearn Niiler of the Scripps Institution of Oceanography in San Diego, the world's leading authority on ocean currents, thinks that there is an even bigger garbage patch in the South Pacific, in the vicinity of Easter Island, but no scientists have yet gone to look. . . .

A Proliferation of Plastic

Look around you. Start counting things made of plastic and don't forget your buttons, the stretch in your underwear, the little caps on the end of your shoelaces. The stuff is absolutely ubiquitous, forming the most basic infrastructure of modern consumer society. We are scarcely out of the womb when we meet our first plastic: wristband, aspirator, thermometer, disposable nappy. We gnaw on plastic teething rings and for the rest of our lives scarcely pass a moment away from plastics.

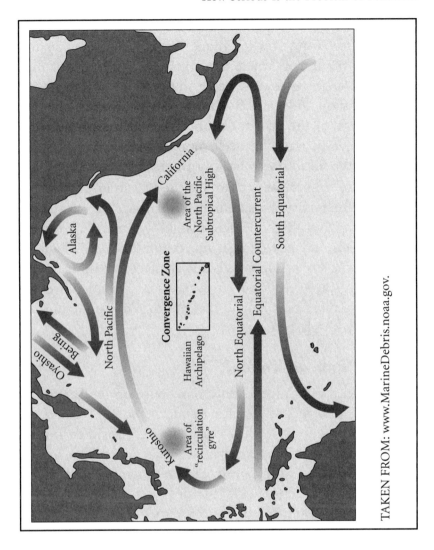

The benefits of plastic, most of which relate to convenience, consumer choice and profit, have been phenomenal. But except for the small percentage that has been incinerated, every single molecule of plastic that has ever been manufactured is still somewhere in the environment, and some 100 million tons of it are floating in the oceans.

A dead albatross was found recently with a piece of plastic from the 1940s in its stomach. Even if plastic production halted tomorrow, the planet would be dealing with its environmental consequences for thousands of years, and on the bottom of the oceans where an estimated 70 percent of marine plastic debris ends up—water bottles sink fairly quickly—for tens of thousands of years. It may form a layer in the geological record of the planet, or some microbe may evolve that can digest plastic and find itself supplied with a vast food resource. In the meantime, what can we do?

What we cannot do is clean up the plastic in the oceans. 'It's the biggest misunderstanding people have on this issue,' Moore says. 'They think the ocean is like a lake and we can go out with nets and just clean it up. People find it difficult to grasp the true size of the oceans and the fact that most of this plastic is in tiny pieces and it's everywhere. All we can do is stop putting more of it in, and that means redesigning our relationship with plastic.'

Getting People to Think

At the far end of a huge loading warehouse on the San Francisco docks dub reggae is pulsing and two young women are shooting dry ice into two-litre plastic bottles. David de Rothschild, the tall, bearded, long-haired, environmentalist son of the Rothschild banking family, wearing hemp Nikes and a skull-and-bones belt buckle, strides in past a display of nurdles, an aquarium full of plastic soup and various rejected prototypes of the catamaran he intends to build and sail across the Pacific to Australia, visiting the Great Pacific Garbage Patch and various rubbish-strewn islands along the way.

He wants the boat to be made entirely out of recycled plastics and float on recycled plastic bottles, and this has presented a daunting challenge to his team of designers, consultants and naval architects. Human ingenuity has devised many fine applications for recycled plastic, but boat-building has not so far been one of them. The design team has had to start from scratch, over and over again. Furthermore, because the point of this voyage is to galvanise media and public attention on the issue of plastic waste, the boat needs to look dramatic and iconic, and it must produce all its own energy, generate no emissions and compost its waste.

'The message of this project is that plastic's not the enemy,' de Rothschild says, speaking rapidly and unstoppably in a mid-Atlantic accent. He is full of bright energy, good humour, marketing slogans and an almost childlike enthusiasm. 'It's about rethinking waste as a resource. It's about doing smart things with plastic and showcasing solutions. It's about using adventure to engage people and start a conversation that creates change in society. You're always going to get people who say, "Oh, he's a bloody Rothschild, sitting on a boat made of, what's that? Champagne bottles?" And that's fine because it gets people talking about it and thinking about where their rubbish goes.' . . .

He decided to name the boat *Plastiki*, in homage to *Kon-Tiki*, the raft of balsa logs and hemp ropes in which Thor Heyerdahl sailed across the Pacific in 1947. He recruited designers, a public relations team and corporate sponsors, including Hewlett-Packard and the International Watch Company. He won't say how much it is costing or how much of his own money is going into it, only that it is more than he would like and less than it could be.

Jo Royle, the renowed British yachtswoman, has signed on as skipper, and two of Thor Heyerdahl's grandchildren have agreed to join the crew. And through Adventure Ecology, de Rothschild has launched a competition called SMART, inviting individuals and organisations from science, marketing, art and industrial design research and technology to present tangible solutions to the problems of plastic waste, and offering grants and publicity to the winners.

Knowing What to Do Is Not Enough

In general terms, it is already clear what we need to do about plastic. Since it is made from oil, which will run out in our lifetimes and get more expensive as it does, we have to start re-using plastic and designing it for re-use. At present only a few of our many hundred plastics can simply be melted down and moulded into something else; the rest are cross-contaminated with other chemicals and types of plastic. But the billion-dollar plastic industry is tooled for virgin plastic and resistant to change.

Charles Moore gives talks to plastic industry executives whenever he can and finds very little interest in recycling, because it's the least profitable sector of the industry. 'A lot of companies and product designers and marketing people don't like recycled plastic either,' de Rothschild says, 'You can't dye it with those bright, attention-grabbing colours.'

For consumers, the easiest way to make a difference is to give up plastic shopping bags and plastic water bottles, which contribute more to plastic pollution than any other products. Then comes plastic packaging, which is a little more complicated. It is easy to point out examples of excessive packaging, but plastic does have the virtue of being lighter than paper, cardboard and glass, which gives it a smaller carbon footprint. For food especially, recyclable plastic packaging is probably the best option. . . .

After another pint, he [de Rothschild] admits to serious doubts—not that the *Plastiki* will get built and complete its voyage, but that it is still possible to save the oceans from ecological collapse. Overfishing is the most urgent problem, but what really scares him and the marine scientists is acidification caused by global warming. The oceans are absorbing more and more of the carbon dioxide that we are putting into the air and it is changing the pH of the water, turning the seas more acid, with potentially catastrophic effects on marine organisms and ecosystems.

'A lot of scientists think we're basically screwed, but what are you going to do?' he asks. 'Enjoy your beer, enjoy your family, make the most of it while it lasts? I think there's a real big movement for that at the moment and part of me understands that. But there's a bigger part of me that says we've got to find a solution, collectively. I mean, come on. We spent $265 billion preparing for the Y2K bug and we didn't even know if it was going to happen or not. We know for an absolute fact that if we continue on our current rate of consumption, we're going to run out of resources. But the annual budget for the United Nations Environment Programme last year [2008] was $190 million. And the budget for the latest James Bond movie was $205 million.'

He chuckles at that, checks his watch and calls for the bill. It is time to walk the dogs and then work the second half of his standard 17-hour day. Outside, he points to San Francisco Bay, looking pristine and lovely in the late afternoon sunshine. 'Maybe that's the trouble,' he says. 'You'd never guess what's under the surface if you didn't know, would you?'

> *"The Great Pacific Garbage Patch . . . has become a symbol. . . . But [it] . . . is hard to measure, and few agree on how big it is or how much plastic it holds."*

The Quantity and Impact of Plastic Debris in the World's Oceans Is Unknown

Carl Bialik

In the following viewpoint, Carl Bialik questions the validity of claims about the enormity of the Great Pacific Garbage Patch, a patch of garbage found in an area where ocean currents converge in the Pacific Ocean. Quantifying the amount of plastic in the garbage patch has proved challenging, he maintains. Indeed, Bialik argues, extrapolating any findings in one area to the entire region is difficult, as the patch's borders shift with the currents. While no patch of plastic floating in the ocean is desirable, misleading the public by exaggerating its size or impact is unproductive, he reasons. Bialik writes The Numbers Guy, a Wall Street Journal *column that examines the way numbers are used and abused.*

Carl Bialik, "How Big Is That Widening Gyre of Floating Plastic?" *Wall Street Journal*, March 25, 2009. Reproduced by permission.

As you read, consider the following questions:

1. In Bialik's opinion, why do researchers survey only a small sample of the gyre for plastic and zooplankton?

2. According to Angelicque White, why might comparing plastic and plankton weight not be an ideal way to measure the problem?

3. In the author's view, why are hard numbers about the impact of plastic on ocean birds and mammals tough to come by?

A soup of plastic debris floats off the coast of California, a testament to humanity's reliance on plastic and the failure to dispose of it properly.

The Great Pacific Garbage Patch

Just how big is this oceanic zone? Some say it is about the size of Quebec, or 600,000 square miles—also described as twice the size of Texas. Others say this expanse of junk swept together by currents is the size of the U.S.—3.8 million square miles. Or, it could be twice that size.

The Great Pacific Garbage Patch, as it has been called, has become a symbol of what some say is a looming crisis over trash. But this floating mass of plastic in the Pacific Ocean is hard to measure, and few agree on how big it is or how much plastic it holds. That makes it difficult to determine what to do about it.

That hasn't stopped activists and the media from using only the biggest estimates of the patch's size to warn of an environmental catastrophe.

"We've found it really captures the public's imagination and its focus," says Eben Schwartz, marine-debris program manager for the California Coastal Commission, a state agency. However, "as hard as [environmental advocates] try to characterize it accurately, it is prone to mischaracterization."

The plastic-rich portion of the ocean is a product of swirling currents, known as the North Pacific Subtropical Gyre, that gather and concentrate debris. It captured public attention thanks to the efforts of Charles Moore, a woodworker-turned-sea captain who sailed through the zone in 1997 and was stunned to find plastic debris hundreds of miles from land. "That set off alarm bells and made me want to monitor it, made me want to quantify it, made me want to get a better handle on it," says Capt. Moore, a licensed merchant-marine officer. He dedicated the Algalita Marine Research Foundation that he had founded to studying this region of the ocean and publicizing its plastic problem.

Researchers at the foundation have attempted to quantify the gyre by sailing deep into the Pacific and trawling for plastic and zooplankton using a contraption that resembles a manta ray. Sifting through the entire gyre for plastic would be impossible, so researchers survey a small sample.

Debating the Size of the Plastic Gyre

But it is difficult to know how to extrapolate their findings to the entire region, or even what that region is. The borders of the gyre shift between seasons, and some scientists, such as Holly Bamford, director of the National Oceanic and Atmospheric Administration's [NOAA's] marine-debris program, argue that the high-plastic area is confined to a relatively small part of the gyre.

"I admire Charles," says David Karl, an oceanographer at the University of Hawaii. But Capt. Moore's estimate of the size of the plastic patch—up to twice the size of the U.S.—strikes Prof. Karl as guesswork. "He doesn't know the edge" of the area.

Capt. Moore has relied on models of ocean currents from a retired NOAA scientist to help estimate the scope of the concentrated-plastic zone, with debris lurking, often in tiny, barely perceptible pieces, at or just below the surface. "I just did a very crude estimate, by getting a globe and placing my hand over the area defined by this current, and placing my hand over the continent of Africa" to see how the two compared, he says. "The condensed-soup part may be considerably less than the whole," he concedes, but he is frustrated by critics who play down the scope of the problem without doing any fieldwork.

Even as the debate over the plastic patch's size continues, some of the foundation's estimates have been reported as scientific certainty. For instance, a decade ago, researchers found that the ratio of plastic to zooplankton by mass was six to one. A more recent visit turned up an increase in this ratio, to 46 to one, according to the foundation's website. But that is an average of the ratio at each testing site, which included some very high ratios, probably anomalies. A more comparable figure is eight to one, representing a more modest increase when results are aggregated across all testing sites.

In addition, comparing plastic and plankton weight might not be an ideal way to measure the problem, according to Angelicque White, a biological oceanographer at the Oregon State University who accompanied Prof. Karl on a recent voyage to the gyre. Dr. White points out that many plankton are too small for the nets, and might not have been included in the count. What's more, while the heaviest bits of plastic inflate the measure of the debris patch, those pieces pose less of an environmental threat, because they are too large for marine creatures to mistake for food.

Capt. Moore said that his scientific papers have made these distinctions clear. But news articles generally haven't. Dr. Bamford says inconsistent units of measurement of the plastic problem have impeded research. "We're trying to develop a standardized method," she says of NOAA, "so we can really get a handle on how this compares to various locations around the world." It's possible that consistent measurement will reveal that other parts of the ocean without a catchy name are just as plastic rich, or more so.

The Dangers of Exaggerating the Research

Some misinformation comes from other environmental groups exaggerating the alarming research. Environmental advocate David Suzuki has written of a "massive, expanding island of plastic debris 30 meters [98 feet] deep and bigger than the province of Quebec." Asked whether the high-plastic region could really be called an island, Bill Wareham, senior marine conservation specialist with the David Suzuki Foundation, says, "It's not going to look like [an] island in the context of, 'Gee, I can walk across that.' But it is a very high density of plastic." He adds, "David speaks in a way where he's framing the issue in a way people can understand it."

Other advocates object to such terminology. "The problem with superlative statements that this is somehow a huge float-ing mass of plastic is that they inevitably lead to desensitizing people when they learn the truth of it," says David Santillo, a senior scientist with Greenpeace.

Even if scientists and advocates could agree on numbers for the size and plastic concentration of the gyre, it is unclear what they would do with the information. Plastics can harm ocean birds and mammals [that] eat it, because they carry toxins, can pierce internal organs and can trick animals into thinking they are full. But hard numbers are tough to come by. "It's so hard to say a bird died due to plastic in its stom-ach," says Dr. Bamford. "We have seen birds mature and live out their whole life, and necropsies show plastic in their stom-ach."

Though no one thinks any possible benefits of plastic out-weigh risks, Prof. Karl did find some positive aspects of the patch—a high concentration of microorganisms clinging to the debris. "The microorganisms are good for the ocean, be-cause it turns out they're making oxygen," Prof. Karl says. "If plastics were otherwise neutral to the environment, then they'd be helping by harvesting more solar energy." Dr. Bamford says it is possible that a cleanup, even if it were feasible, would do more harm than good, by removing these organisms.

Capt. Moore says quantifying the plastic could provide a starting point for measuring the effectiveness of land-based efforts to choke the flow of plastic to ocean waters. "I would love to have a government agency form a concerted program to quantify the debris," he says. "It's a tragedy of the commons: Nobody owns the problem."

> "Of the 60 pharmaceuticals the [US Geological Survey] was testing for, it found 30 of them in 139 streams in 30 states."

Pharmaceuticals May Be Poisoning America's Drinking Water

Patricia Frank

A growing number of pharmaceutical compounds are showing up in America's drinking water, claims Patricia Frank in the following viewpoint. More Americans than ever are being treated with prescription drugs that often end up in wastewater facilities that are not designed to filter out these compounds of emerging concern (CECs), she maintains. As a result, Frank asserts, fish found close to watershed and wastewater discharge areas show reproductive abnormalities, which is raising concerns about the impact of CECs on human health. Growing public concern may pressure wastewater treatment facilities to find ways to safely remove CECs from America's drinking water, she contends. Frank is a freelance writer and editor of Vibrant Village.

Patricia Frank, "The Next Drug Problem," *American City & County*, June 1, 2007. Reproduced by permission of Penton Media.

As you read, consider the following questions:

1. What did a USGS analysis of a sample of smallmouth bass found in the Potomac basin and the Shenandoah watershed reveal?

2. According to the author, what are some of the techniques for removing compounds from drinking water?

3. In the author's view, what evidence is there that the public seems ready to address the issue of pharmaceuticals in America's drinking water?

Hidden among the well-known problems faced by water professionals—aging infrastructure, dwindling supply—is another emerging issue: rising amounts of pharmaceutical compounds in surface water and drinking water. And, considering the increasing numbers of people being treated with drugs at earlier ages and an aging population taking multiple medications for a variety of health conditions, more of those compounds likely will find their way into the nation's wastewater facilities.

Early signs of the problem were discovered in U.S. Geological Survey (USGS) research in 1999. Of the 60 pharmaceuticals the agency was testing for, it found 30 of them in 139 streams in 30 states. In addition, 80 percent of the streams had one or more contaminants, 54 percent had five or more, and 13 percent showed 20 or more.

"We can measure over 150 compounds in water alone," says Dana Kolpin, a research hydrologist and member of the USGS study team. "Now, the big question is, what kind of environmental consequences [do they pose] to terrestrial and aquatic ecosystems and, maybe in the long term, even human health. We just don't know what the exposure risk is to many of these compounds."

Determining the Effects

Scientists from the Iowa City, Iowa-based USGS, other government agencies and universities are attempting to determine the potential effects of chronic exposure to pharmaceutical mixtures—otherwise known as Compounds of Emerging Concern (CECs)—such as endocrine disruption and the development of antibiotic resistance, in the aquatic environment, soil, plants, animals and humans.

Though the amounts being measured often are in parts per million or parts per billion, many of the compounds are designed to have effects at low levels. "These CECs are active at very, very low concentrations in the water and in the sediments," says Jeff Armstrong, senior scientist in the ocean monitoring group for the Orange County, Calif. Sanitation District. "It's not so much the death of the animals [that is a concern], it is reproductive effects or effects on other areas of the endocrine system, the ability to fight off infection or other aspects of reproduction."

Endocrine disruptors are chemicals that mimic or block hormones or trigger abnormal reproductive responses in fish and possibly in humans. Nevertheless, our ability to measure the compounds is ahead of our knowledge of their long-term effects.

Increasing Sexual Abnormalities

However, some fish in close proximity to wastewater discharge points exhibit multiple sexual abnormalities, such as male fish with deformed testes or low or no sperm counts, for example. Some fish are classified as "intersex" with sex characteristics of both genders. Kolpin says a large proportion of the male fish have either female egg protein or female characteristics.

Following a high number of fish deaths in the Potomac [River] basin and the Shenandoah watershed between 2003 and 2005, the USGS and scientists from Virginia and West Virginia analyzed samples of 30 smallmouth bass from six sites. A microscopic examination of the fish testes discovered 42 percent of the male bass had developed eggs. A second USGS study found an even higher number of intersex fish— 79 percent. "[In the Potomac, we found] a big portion of the male fish having either female egg yolk protein or female characteristics," Kolpin says. Douglas Chambers, the study's lead scientist, says that all water samples contained detectable levels of at least one known endocrine-disrupting compound.

Pacific Ocean flatfish found in sediment near Orange County, Calif.'s Huntington Beach effluent discharge point exhibited similar effects. "We're finding that male fish are producing [endocrine-disrupting compounds] in concentrations that normal males should not," Armstrong says. "That means they're being exposed to some kind of estrogenic compound. We're finding the fish near our outfall and [the estrogenic compound] seems to be in higher concentrations [there, which indicates] that something's coming out in the treated wastewater that might be causing this."

"It's really not certain what's going on, but [there is no doubt] that there is evidence of endocrine-type biomarkers in fish downstream from wastewater outfalls," says Shane Snyder, research and development project manager for the Southern Nevada Water Authority in Las Vegas. "The degree of magnitude of the effect seems like it's going to be related to the treatment type, the degree of mixing and the mobility of the fish."

The Sources and Treatment of CECs

The contaminants may originate from hospitals and medical facilities, vet clinics, pharmaceutical manufacturers, and people using prescription and over-the-counter medications and personal care products. "[Medical facilities] can be a big source of . . . pharmaceuticals, X-ray and MRI contrast agents and chemotherapy drugs," Kolpin says. "Maybe they need to have separate wastewater treatment so they're not just put in with residential waste."

Designed to remove conventional pollutants, such as suspended solids and easily biodegradable organic materials, most conventional wastewater treatment plants do not remove CECs. The concentration of the compounds that remain in wastewater treatment plant effluent depends on the type of treatment, the specific compounds as well as the concentration in the influent entering the plant.

Techniques for removing compounds from drinking water include advanced oxidation, membrane filtration and filtration with granular activated carbon, and nano-filtration combined with reverse osmosis, which eliminates all the drugs. Each technology serves a function, but each can produce an unwelcome side effect.

Conventional ozone renders certain CECs inactive, but its use comes with a price, Snyder warns. "Ozone creates regulated by-products—regulated on cancer endpoints. [It's] great [that] you're putting in ozone, but what about all the cancer-causing by-products they form?"

Chlorine, the most commonly used wastewater disinfectant in the U.S., is the least effective in removing CECs.

Kolpin's concern is the creation of chlorination by-products. The EPA [Environmental Protection Agency] already has set drinking water standards of 100 parts per billion for one group of by-products, called trihalomethanes, because of their potential to cause cancer. "You may be removing the parent compound [of CECs] but creating these chlorinated degradation products, [and you] may be worse off than when you started," he says. "Certainly chlorination has the advantages of removing pathogens, but to say that's the best route to remove [CECs needs to be researched]."

Reverse osmosis (RO) uses large amounts of electricity and produces a highly concentrated wastewater stream. "[RO] creates a stream of concentrated waste, [so] what do you do with the concentrated waste stream that you've generated?" Snyder says.

Techniques that combine ozone and granular activated carbon (GAC) are effective for removing industrial and agricultural pollutants, and also improve the water's taste and odor. The filters get dirty and must be washed periodically, otherwise the water can become infected with *cryptosporidium* or *Giardia*.

The Challenge of Identifying CECs

Before water utilities can choose an effective technology, though, the harmful CECs have to be identified. "First we need to figure out, 'Do we need to mitigate?' And, if we do, then we'll address those larger issues of how to do it," Armstrong says.

Still, common wastewater treatments can be useful in removing CECs. "The tertiary treatment, like reverse osmosis (RO) or micro- or nano-filtration, removes pretty much 100 percent of [CECs]," Armstrong says. "There's a lot in the literature that [says] ozonation renders these [compounds] biologically inactive. The problem is doing that on a large scale. [We process] 255 million gallons a day. There's no way we can do that, so we have to look to other ways to figure out what kind of mitigation strategy's going to work for us."

CECs will not be regulated in the near future, at least. "Due to insufficient data [on the occurrence and toxicity], it appears that pharmaceuticals will not be regulated any time soon," says Snyder, who works with the EPA on its Contaminant Candidate List 3 (CCL3). The substances that will be regulated, however, will be available next summer.

Meanwhile, the Las Vegas [Valley] Water District has added ozone to its expanded wastewater treatment facility. Ozone was chosen for its disinfection power to prevent a repeat of a 1994 *cryptosporidium* outbreak in the city that was linked to 32 deaths, as well as for its ability to eliminate CECs. "Ozone is extremely effective for destroying estrogenicity, and that's where our concern lies for the fish," Snyder says.

The Use of Take-Back Programs

Because 50 percent to 90 percent of ingested drugs are excreted, state and local governments are attempting to involve the public through drug take-back programs to stem the flow at one of its source points. "We'll deal with that in the treatment plants as best we can, but keeping the extraneous pharmaceuticals out of the environment is where the majority of the action seems to be at the municipal level today," Armstrong says.

State legislators, too, are becoming more aware of drinking water being contaminated with prescription drugs. California's Senate Bill 966, requiring every pharmaceutical drug retailer to collect out-of-date drugs for proper disposal, made its way through two committees before being voted down in May.

The public also seems ready to address the issue. In May 2006, the San Francisco Bay Area Pollution Prevention Group collected 3,634 pounds of pharmaceutical waste from 1,500 residents, and South Portland, Maine, recently sponsored a one-day event and collected 55,000 pills. The state's legislators currently are exploring instituting turn-in, mail-back and other disposal programs.

Making it convenient for the public to participate in drug take-back programs appears to be helping. San Mateo County, Calif., featured repainted (and donated) U.S. Postal Service mailboxes, which made their program as easy to access as mailing a letter. Their pilot program in four locations collected nearly 590 pounds of unwanted drugs in just four months, at a cost of $924, plus the costs of the police to collect the drugs.

Despite the best efforts to control the drugs that enter the wastewater stream, water utilities still can expect challenges to meet growing needs and the delivery of safe drinking water to their customers, including removing CECs. "I'm hoping if we are able to identify certain compounds that seem to be the culprits in potential human health risks, that technology could be developed to mitigate those, rather than take out everything," Snyder says. "People have the perception that utilities like ours pull from some giant coffer of money and we can do whatever we want to get down to the last nanogram [of contaminant], but the public will pay."

Periodical and Internet Sources Bibliography

The following articles have been selected to supplement the diverse views presented in this chapter.

Sarah Baldauf	"Air Pollution: It's Not Just Your Lungs That Suffer," *U.S. News & World Report*, February 26, 2010.
Chris Baskind	"5 Reasons Not to Drink Bottled Water," Mother Nature Network, March 15, 2010. www.mnn.com.
John M. Broder	"Greenhouse Gases Imperil Health, E.P.A. Announces," *New York Times*, December 7, 2009.
Mark Dorfman and Kirsten Sinclair Rosselot	*Testing the Waters: A Guide to Water Quality at Vacation Beaches*, National Resources Defense Council, 2010.
Charles Duhigg	"Debating How Much Weed Killer Is Safe in Your Water Glass," *New York Times*, August 22, 2009.
Fletcher Harper	"Silence, God, and the Gulf Coast Oil Spill," *Huffington Post*, May 7, 2010.
Michael McCarthy	"The Big Question: How Big Is the Problem of Electronic Waste, and Can It Be Tackled?" *Independent* (UK), February 24, 2010.
Russell McLendon	"What Is the Great Pacific Ocean Garbage Patch?" Mother Nature Network, February 24, 2010. www.mnn.com.
Science Daily	"Water Should Be a Human Right, Experts Argue," June 29, 2009.
Nancy Stoner and Jon Devine	"Facing Up to Freshwater Pollution," *American Prospect*, May 27, 2008.

CHAPTER 2

What Technologies Will Best Reduce Pollution?

Chapter Preface

Many believe that using low-sulfur coal to generate electricity is a promising technology in the effort to reduce air pollution. Low-sulfur coal can be found in the Appalachian Mountains of West Virginia, eastern Kentucky, southwestern Virginia, and some parts of Tennessee. In areas where the coal seams are found just below the surface, coal can be exposed by using bulldozers to remove rock and soil. However, this approach is ineffective in the Appalachian Mountains. To expose low-sulfur coal seams in areas with narrow hills and steep valleys requires the removal of the tops of mountains. Millions of pounds of explosives are used to blast away the rock. In some cases, the elevation of these mountains is reduced by hundreds of feet. Moreover, to maintain access to the coal, the removed material is dumped into nearby valleys. Thus despite the viability of low-sulfur coal as an effective technology to reduce air pollution, many experts point to the negative environmental impact of mountaintop mining as a strong argument against this approach.

The Environmental Protection Agency (EPA) reports that between 1992 and 2002, mountain mining and valley fills (MTM/VF) buried as much as twelve hundred miles of headwater streams that feed major rivers. The EPA also concluded that MTM/VF would affect as many as 1,250 square miles of Appalachian forests between 1992 and 2012. The region is home to native plants, animals, and fish that "have been profoundly altered over the past few centuries and are becoming increasingly threatened," according to the EPA in 2005. Because many scientists fear that MTM/VF poses a threat to the unique ecology of the region and, in turn, the life of the people who live there, some local groups and grassroots organizations are calling for a ban on mountaintop removal mining. Indeed, the impact of mountaintop removal on the environment and local communities is one of several controversies in the debate about which technologies best reduce pollution.

Those who oppose mountaintop mining believe that its impact on the people who live in nearby communities is significant. Judy Bonds of the Coal River Mountain Watch (CRMW), a group of concerned West Virginia citizens, tells her story in the *Charleston Gazette*, a West Virginia newspaper. According to Bonds, mountaintop removal fills local streams with sediment, which increases runoff from steep slopes, which in turn leads to flooding miles downstream. "I know people who sleep in their street clothes at night because they've been through flooding and worry about having to run again in the middle of the night," Bonds explains in the 2007 article. She also complains that mountaintop mining breaks windows and cracks foundations. Mine runoff and selenium discharges have also contaminated West Virginia rivers and streams. Not only do people who live in affected areas now have to pay for public water access, but "we can't even swim in our own streams anymore," Bonds explains.

Mining regulators at the Office of Surface Mining Reclamation and Enforcement (OSM) claim that since the enactment of the Surface Mining Control and Reclamation Act (SMCRA) in 1977, mining is more strictly regulated than in the past. In testimony before the House Committee on Natural Resources on July 25, 2007, Stephanie Timmermeyer, West Virginia secretary of environmental protection, said "although there are still impacts from mining, the practice is now carefully planned and permitted with extensive scientific, regulatory and public input." The West Virginia Coal Association adds that mountaintop removal accounted for about 16 percent of national coal production and thus should be an important part of any energy program.

Even mountaintop removal critics agree that replacing energy sources as demand continues to rise will not be easy. Indeed, analysts on both sides of the mountaintop removal debate continue to make their cases in the courthouse and in the court of public opinion. The authors in the following chapter explore similar concerns in the debate over the effectiveness of other technologies designed to reduce pollution.

> *"[Clean coal] technology could reduce coal plant carbon dioxide emissions to the atmosphere by more than 90 percent."*

Clean Coal Technologies Can Reduce Carbon Dioxide Emissions

Robert S. Giglio

Since today's energy policies must balance stimulating the economy and protecting the environment, policy makers should invest in clean coal technology, claims Robert S. Giglio in the following viewpoint. Given that coal is the world's most abundant energy source, clean coal technologies may help meet growing energy demands, he reasons. While burning coal for electricity creates pollution, carbon capture and storage (CCS) technologies can significantly reduce these pollutants and their impact on the environment, Giglio argues. In fact, he asserts, preliminary testing reveals that CCS can reduce carbon dioxide emissions by more than 90 percent. Giglio is the director of global marketing and strategy for the Foster Wheeler Global Power Group, an energy equipment provider.

Robert S. Giglio, "Clean Coal: What Works Now and Tomorrow," *Environmental Protection*, October 19, 2009. Reproduced by permission.

As you read, consider the following questions:

1. Giglio questions if the energy programs outlined so far will meet 2050 energy goals. Explain the reasons behind his concern.

2. Why does the US Energy Information Administration forecast that more coal and natural gas are likely to be used than other energy sources?

3. In the author's view, what are the two main reasons why coal is the best energy source? What are the negatives in using coal?

Diversifying energy sources is a key goal set out in the [Barack] Obama-[Joe] Biden New Energy for America plan. Since taking over the reins of power, the new administration proposed a comprehensive plan to

- invest in alternative and renewable energy,

- end U.S. addiction to foreign oil,

- address the global climate crisis, and

- create thousands of new green energy jobs.

Supporting these goals is more than $150 billion over 10 years in clean energy and energy efficiency projects in the president's budget and a commitment to make the research and experimentation tax credit permanent. The administration expects investments in research and development today to pay off in high-quality green jobs tomorrow.

Despite these positive steps, the overall energy policy goals are extremely ambitious. Can the United States reduce its greenhouse gas (GHG) emissions by 80 percent by 2050? It is questionable whether the programs outlined so far will be able to meet these energy goals, especially in light of the current recession.

Some voices say that President Obama must strike a balance between stimulating the economy in the next few years and investing in the long-term future of the environment. One way to do that is to focus on reducing environmental impacts while improving technologies so they evolve into long-term solutions for reducing GHG emissions.

A Role for Coal

Energy Secretary Steven Chu, PhD, told the Committee on Energy and Natural Resources in January [2009] that, among other things, clean coal is a necessary element in planning for the future and more investment is needed for carbon capture and storage (CCS) research. CCS refers to capturing carbon dioxide (one of the earth's most abundant GHGs) from coal-fired power plants, compressing it and storing it underground, in deep-saline aquifers or other geologic formations.

The Obama-Biden administration supports incentives to accelerate investment in zero-carbon coal facilities, and the policy includes developing coal-fired plants with CCS.

A unique steam generator technology, circulating fluidized bed (CFB) reactors may have a place in meeting the goals of the U.S. energy plan. They offer an efficient way to burn coal alone or in combination with biomass, capturing pollutants and transforming the fuel's heat into the steam used to produce power.

CFB uses fluidization technology to mix and circulate fuel particles with limestone as they burn in a low-temperature combustion process. The combination of limestone and low-burning temperature removes pollutants or minimizes their formation during the burning process. Vertical-tube, super-critical steam technology allows more of the fuel's energy to be transferred to the steam, improving overall efficiency and reducing the amount of fuel needed to generate electricity and reducing air emissions.

Due to its unique combustion process, CFBs can burn such biomass fuels as forest residue, demolition wood, sawdust, corn husks, and sugarcane. Biomass is considered carbon neutral, since it absorbs and stores carbon from the atmosphere during its growth cycle through photosynthesis. When burned, biomass releases the same carbon back to the atmosphere, resulting in nearly zero net carbon dioxide emissions to the atmosphere.

A Bridge Between Fuel Sources

Power plants don't burn only biomass because this fuel source's supply chain is undeveloped, limiting the size of such plants to about 25–50 megawatts electrical (MWe). Under the current situation, 10 or more biomass plants would have to be built to generate a more conventional large-scale (300 MWe or larger) power plant. The scale and fuel supply limitations drives up the cost of a biomass plant 20 to 30 percent higher than that from conventional large fossil power plants. The CFB technology provides a bridge from strictly coal as a fuel source to a combination of coal and biomass that meets large-scale power demands. It can use more biomass when available or fall back on coal when it is not. This can be done today, while still producing affordable electricity. . . .

But what about those coal power days? New flexible combustion technologies currently under development hold promise for lowering both the cost and technology risk for the CCS solution. These technologies simplify the carbon dioxide capture and removal process by using a mixture of oxygen and recycled CFB flue gas to produce a carbon dioxide-rich flue gas that can be more easily captured. The technology could reduce coal plant carbon dioxide emissions to the atmosphere by more than 90 percent, according to pilot testing and demonstrations.

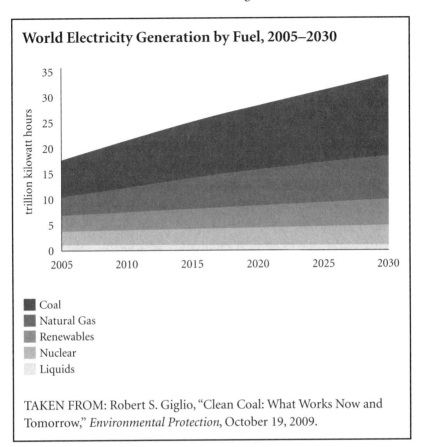

World Electricity Generation by Fuel, 2005–2030

- Coal
- Natural Gas
- Renewables
- Nuclear
- Liquids

TAKEN FROM: Robert S. Giglio, "Clean Coal: What Works Now and Tomorrow," *Environmental Protection*, October 19, 2009.

Demand and Supply

Obama's plan addresses a broad range of energy users, but the one area where this subject hits closest to home—literally—is in the way electric companies generate power for residential use. Coal is the lowest cost energy source for U.S. residences. Its use will steady energy prices at a time when investment and growth is needed to [stimulate] the economy.

At home and abroad, the government predicts the energy demand will only grow. The U.S. Department of Energy, Energy Information Administration (EIA) forecasts that the demand between now and 2030 will increase by 50 percent, with two-thirds of the new demand likely coming from developing nations. To meet these demands, countries around the world will need to tap deeper into all the primary energy sources, including nuclear, natural gas, coal, and renewables.

The EIA forecasts show that, in the coming years, more coal and more natural gas [are] likely to be used than other sources because of their low cost, abundance, and lengthy supply life, coal specifically. Nuclear energy will be constrained by the time it takes to build plants, get regulatory approvals, and by perceived safety concerns. Biofuels and renewable alternatives (for example, wind and solar power) will grow rapidly but will remain a relatively small contributor and will not replace significant quantities of fossil fuels in the near future.

Our nation faces critical challenges in meeting the demand for affordable power in an era of economic uncertainty, when stimulating growth is at the top of the priority list. How can we move forward with this need to keep energy prices affordable while at the same time making progress on the ambitious environmental agenda that includes diversifying our energy sources, improving the environment, and reducing the effects of climate change? We will need to use all the tools in our arsenal, including relying on existing technologies that can provide environmentally friendly power at a cost we can handle.

What About Coal?

Coal is the most abundant primary energy source in the world, capable of supporting U.S. energy needs for more than 300 years at our current usage rate as compared to oil or natural gas, which is projected to be exhausted in about 30–50 years.

It is located in or near the largest population centers and largest industrialized countries like the United States, the United Kingdom, Germany, China, and India. It can also be easily transported and produces among the most reliable and affordable electricity today.

It also carries a significant environmental cost with its use. When coal is burned to produce electricity, it emits air pollutants in the form of oxides of sulfur, nitrogen and carbon into the atmosphere. The oxides of sulfur and nitrogen can contribute to acid rain and smog. And the oxide of carbon in the form of carbon dioxide (CO_2) is a greenhouse gas that can contribute to global warming.

| *"Clean coal: Never was there an oxymoron more insidious, or more dangerous to our public health."*

Clean Coal Technology Will Not Reduce Air Pollution

Jeff Biggers

In the following viewpoint, Jeff Biggers argues that clean coal technologies will not make coal clean. Not only does coal production release dangerous pollutants into America's air and water, but coal mining and transportation also have led to innumerable injuries and deaths, he maintains. Moreover, Biggers asserts, strip mining is leveling Appalachia's mountains and destroying its forests. Coal remains a dirty, dangerous, and destructive way to create energy, he claims. Biggers, the grandson of a coal miner from southern Illinois, is author of Reckoning at Eagle Creek: The Secret Legacy of Coal in the Heartland.

As you read, consider the following questions:

1. What does Burl call the blue marks and bits of coal that Bigger's grandfather had buried in his face?

2. According to the author, what slogan has blindsided any meaningful progress toward a sustainable energy policy?

Jeff Biggers, "'Clean' Coal? Don't Try to Shovel That," *Washington Post*, March 2, 2008. Reproduced by permission.

3. What does the author say is the equivalent of the thousands of tons of explosives set off in Appalachian communities every year?

Every time I hear our political leaders talk about "clean coal," I think about Burl, an irascible old coal miner in West Virginia. After 35 years underground, he struggled to conjure enough breath to match his storytelling verve, as if the iron hoops of a whiskey barrel had been strapped around his lungs. In 1983, during my first visit to Appalachia as a young man, Burl rolled up his pants and showed me the leg that had been mangled in a mining accident. The scars snaked down to his ankles.

"My grandpa barely survived an accident in the mines in southern Illinois," I told him. "He had these blue marks and bits of coal buried in his face."

"Coal tattoo," Burl wheezed. "Don't let anyone ever tell you that coal is clean."

An Insidious Oxymoron

Clean coal: Never was there an oxymoron more insidious, or more dangerous to our public health. Invoked as often by the Democratic presidential candidates as by the Republicans and by liberals and conservatives alike, this slogan has blindsided any meaningful progress toward a sustainable energy policy.

Democrats excoriated President Bush last month [February 2008] when he released a budget calling for more—billions more—in funds to reduce carbon emissions from coal-burning power plants to create "clean coal." But hardly a hoot could be heard about his proposed cuts to more practical investments in solar energy, hydrogen fuel and home energy efficiency.

Meanwhile, leading Democrats were up in arms over the Energy Department's recent decision to abandon the $1.8 billion FutureGen project in eastern Illinois, planned as the first coal-fired plant to capture and store harmful carbon dioxide emissions. Energy Department officials, unlike politicians, had to confront the spiraling costs of this fantasy.

The Dirty Realities

Orwellian language has led to Orwellian politics. With the imaginary vocabulary of "clean coal," too many Democrats and Republicans, as well as a surprising number of environmentalists, have forgotten the dirty realities of extracting coal from the earth. Pummeled by warnings that global warming is triggering the apocalypse, Americans have fallen for the ruse of futuristic science that is clean coal. And in the meantime, swaths of the country are being destroyed before our eyes.

Here's the hog-killing reality that a coal miner like Bud or my grandfather knew firsthand: No matter how "cap 'n trade" schemes pan out in the distant future for coal-fired plants, strip mining and underground coal mining remain the dirtiest and most destructive ways of making energy.

Coal ain't clean. Coal is deadly.

More than 104,000 miners in America have died in coal mines since 1900. Twice as many have died from black lung disease. Dangerous pollutants, including mercury, filter into our air and water. The injuries and deaths caused by overburdened coal trucks are innumerable. Yet even on the heels of a recent report revealing that in the last six years the Mine Safety and Health Administration decided not to assess fines for more than 4,000 violations, Bush administration officials have called for cutting mine safety funds by 6.5 percent. Have they already forgotten the coal miners who were entombed underground in Utah last summer [2007]?

Aboveground, millions of acres across 36 states have been dynamited, torn and churned into bits by strip mining in the last 150 years. More than 60 percent of all coal mined in the United States today, in fact, comes from strip mines.

The Consequences of Coal

260 million	Gallons of water used for coal mining in the U.S. every day
120 million	Tons of solid wastes produced every year by burning coal
90 million	Gallons of waste slurry produced every year while preparing coal to be burned
21 million	People in the U.S. who live within five miles of a coal-fired power plant
12 million	Gallons of water used per hour at an average coal-fired power plant
12,000	Miners who died from black lung disease between 1992 and 2002
1,200+	Miles of streams that have been buried or polluted in Appalachia because of mountaintop removal mining
47	U.S. states and territories with mercury fish consumption advisories for at least some of their waters
150+	New coal-fired power plants proposed for the U.S.
55	Percent decrease in number of coal miners employed from 1985–2000
22	Percent increase in coal mining production from 1985–2005

TAKEN FROM: Sierra Club, *The Dirty Truth About Coal*, June 2007.

The Leveling of Appalachia

In the "United States of Coal," Appalachia has become the poster child for strip mining's worst depravations, which come in the form of mountaintop removal. An estimated 750,000 to 1 million acres of hardwood forests, a thousand miles of waterways and more than 470 mountains and their surrounding communities—an area the size of Delaware—have been erased from the southeastern mountain range in the last two decades. Thousands of tons of explosives—the equivalent of several Hiroshima atomic bombs—are set off in Appalachian communities every year.

How can anyone call this clean?

When the [George W.] Bush administration announced a plan last year to do away with a poorly enforced 1983 regulation that protected streams from being buried by strip-mining waste—one of the last ramparts protecting some of the nation's oldest forests and communities—tens of thousands of people wrote to the Office of Surface Mining [Reclamation and Enforcement] in outrage. Citizens' groups also effectively halted the proposed construction of 59 coal-fired plants in the past year. Yet at last weekend's meeting of the National Governors Association, Democratic and Republican governors once again joined forces, ignored the disastrous reality of mining and championed the chimera of clean coal. Pennsylvania Gov. Ed Rendell even declared that coal states will be "back in business big time."

How much more death and destruction will it take to strip coal of this bright, shining "clean" lie?

As Burl might have said, if our country can rally to save Arctic polar bears from global warming, perhaps Congress can pass the Endangered Appalachians Act to save American miners, their children and their communities from ruin by a reckless industry.

Or at least stop talking about "clean coal."

> *"Plug-in cars ... produce less global warming pollution, emit little or no pollution from the tailpipe, and reduce our dependence on oil."*

Plug-in Electric Vehicles Will Reduce Air Pollution

Siena Kaplan, Brad Heavner, and Rob Sargent

In the following viewpoint, Siena Kaplan, Brad Heavner, and Rob Sargent claim that plug-in cars, which have an electric motor and a battery that can be charged externally, will produce less air pollution over the long term. To achieve these results, they maintain, the electricity supplied to plug-in cars must be clean. At present, the authors assert, some parts of the country generate electricity from coal, which is not a clean energy source. As investment in clean energy sources increases, the authors reason, the pollution-reduction benefits of the plug-in will in turn increase. Kaplan, Heavner, and Sargent represent, respectively, the Frontier Group, Environment Maryland Research & Policy Center, and Environment America Research & Policy Center, environmental advocacy organizations.

Siena Kaplan, Brad Heavner, and Rob Sargent, "Charging Ahead: Curbing Oil Consumption with Plug-in Cars," Environment Maryland Research and Policy Center, June 2010, pp. 7–14. Reproduced by permission.

As you read, consider the following questions:

1. According to Kaplan, Heavner, and Sargent, how many studies show that plug-in cars produce less carbon dioxide than traditional gasoline-powered cars?

2. What did the study by the University of California, Berkeley, Center for Entrepreneurship & Technology predict about global warming emission reductions from plug-in cars?

3. What did an EPRI and NRDC study predict would be the result if 40 percent of the vehicles on the road in 2030 were plug-in hybrids?

The term "plug-in" refers to any car that has both an electric motor and a battery that can be charged externally. A plug-in hybrid is a car with both an electric motor and an internal combustion engine. Plug-in hybrids are similar to conventional hybrids, except that they have larger batteries that can be charged externally, allowing them to achieve in the range of 100 miles per gallon of gasoline. Electric cars run entirely on electricity, with no internal combustion engine.

The Advantages of Plug-in Cars

Plug-in cars have several advantages over gasoline-powered vehicles. They produce less global warming pollution, emit little or no pollution from the tailpipe, and reduce our dependence on oil. Battery-powered vehicles also have practical and environmental advantages over many other types of alternative-fuel vehicles.

While plug-in cars are not yet cost competitive with gasoline-powered vehicles and the technology still needs improvement, they are ready today for consumers who are eager to drive low emission cars. . . .

The size and scope of the benefits America would receive from plug-in vehicles depend, however, on how we generate the electricity to supply them. If we clean up the electric grid by reducing our use of polluting energy sources and increasing our use of clean energy sources such as wind and solar power, we can maximize the environmental benefits of plug-in vehicles.

Global Warming and Plug-ins

Plug-in cars emit less global warming pollution than cars powered by gasoline when fueled from today's electricity sources. This is largely because electric motors are vastly more efficient than the internal combustion engine, driving a car much farther on the same amount of energy.

Many studies have compared global warming pollution from plug-ins versus that from conventional cars. There is a wide range of results, since there are a number of factors that differ from study to study—for example, the gas mileage of the conventional cars plug-ins are being compared against, and the amount of electricity the plug-in cars are assumed to use. However, over 40 recent studies have shown that plug-in cars produce less carbon dioxide than traditional gasoline-powered cars.

An electric car powered by electricity from today's electric grid will have lower global warming emissions than a conventional car. One study by the Pacific Northwest National Laboratory (PNNL) found that a car fueled by electricity from unused capacity in our current electric system would emit 27 percent less global warming pollution than a car fueled by gasoline.

The environmental benefits of plug-ins depend on the source of electricity used to power them. Because some parts of the country are heavily reliant on coal—which produces large amounts of global warming pollution—and others use cleaner sources of energy, the benefits of plug-ins vary from state to state and region to region. Even with this variation, the PNNL study found that global warming emissions per

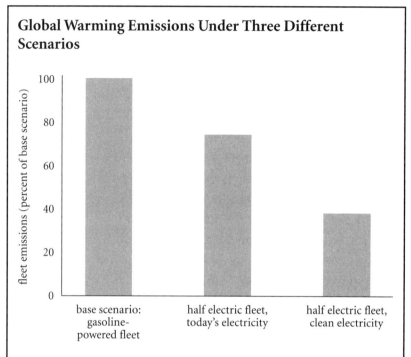

Global Warming Emissions Under Three Different Scenarios

fleet emissions (percent of base scenario)

base scenario: gasoline-powered fleet

half electric fleet, today's electricity

half electric fleet, clean electricity

"Base scenario" assumes an average fuel economy of 35 miles per gallon and high gasoline prices; "half electric fleet" is 46 percent of the current U.S. fleet powered by electricity; "today's electricity" is power from the 2007 electric grid; "clean electricity" is electricity with zero global warming emissions.

TAKEN FROM: Siena Kaplan, Brad Heavner, and Rob Sargent, "Charging Ahead: Curbing Oil Consumption with Plug-in Cars," Environment Maryland Research & Policy Center, June 2010.

mile driven by an electric motor would be lower in every area of the country except for the Northern Plains states, where emissions would stay the same.

In other words, cars driving on electric power deliver roughly the same level of global warming emission reductions as today's conventional hybrids—with greater reductions in areas of the country with a cleaner electric grid and smaller reductions in areas with a dirtier grid. So why bother with a new technology that is (for the time being at least) more expensive than today's hybrids?

A Need for Clean Electricity

The reason is that plug-ins are among the few technologies capable of producing dramatic reductions in global warming pollution from vehicles over the long term. Plug-ins can achieve that potential if they draw their power from a clean electricity grid, or from solar panels on rooftops or parking lots.

A study by the University of California, Berkeley, Center for Entrepreneurship & Technology showed that having clean electricity sources would increase the global warming emission reductions from plug-in cars. The study found that if about half of the U.S. fleet were powered by clean electricity in 2030, total fleet emissions would be reduced by 62 percent—compared with a fleet powered with high-priced gasoline and with an average fuel economy of 35 miles per gallon. By contrast, if the same electric vehicles were powered by electricity from the 2007 U.S. grid, fleet emissions would be reduced only 26 percent.

In fact, beyond just utilizing clean energy, plug-in cars could actually make it easier to increase the amount of clean energy in the United States. With the implementation of smart grid technology, the storage capacity in plug-in cars could be tapped to smooth out the intermittency of renewable energy sources such as wind and solar power. By expanding the grid's ability to accommodate renewable sources of energy, plug-ins could contribute to reducing global warming emissions in the United States even when they are parked.

Air Quality and Plug-ins

Switching to plug-in cars would improve air quality for most people in the United States. If the nation continues to rely on coal-fired power plants, emissions may rise for some people who live near those plants. But enforcing stringent air pollution standards for power plants and increasing the amount of clean electricity would reduce that threat and ensure that a switch to plug-in cars would improve air quality for everyone.

Plug-in cars produce less tailpipe pollution than conventional cars, but fueling them with electricity from our current energy sources will increase air pollution from power plants. A study by the Department of Energy's Pacific Northwest National Laboratory found that powering a car with electricity would result in 93 percent less smog-forming volatile organic compounds (VOCs) and 31 percent less nitrogen oxides (NO_x) than powering a car with gasoline power, including power plant emissions. Further reductions would likely occur if polluting sources of electricity generation were to be replaced with cleaner, renewable sources.

These estimates assume, however, that we would use existing coal-fired power plants, as they are, to supply the extra electricity for our cars. While coal plants will always be dirty, technology exists that limits the amount of soot and smog they produce. Power plant emissions of NO_x and SO_x [sulfur oxide] are limited by a national cap-and-trade program which reduces some power plant emissions over time. As the number of plug-in cars increases over time, our electric grid will continue to become cleaner in regard to air quality as long as we enforce and strengthen the laws that we have in place.

A study by the Electric Power Research Institute (EPRI) and Natural Resources Defense Council (NRDC) showed that using plug-in cars will improve air quality beyond the large emissions reductions that will already result from current laws. The study found that if 40 percent of the vehicles on the road were plug-in hybrids in 2030, VOC and NO_x emissions would be reduced by over 1.5 percent, compared with continuing to use conventional vehicles. Sulfur oxide (SO_x) emissions would not rise or fall compared with business as usual.

Limiting Power Plant Pollution

Pollution from power plants can have serious impacts on nearby communities, as well as the environment as a whole. But fossil fuel–burning power plants tend to be located in less populated areas, whereas automobile pollution is greatest in the midst of densely populated urban areas. As a result, when weighted for population, the clean air benefits of plug-ins are even more significant. The EPRI and NRDC study found that if 40 percent of the vehicles on the road were plug-in hybrids in 2030 and current power plant pollution laws were enforced, smog levels would decrease for 61 percent of the population, and increase for 1 percent of the population. Soot would decrease for 82 percent of the population, and increase for 3 percent of the population.

As plug-in vehicles make up an increasingly large percentage of our cars, it will be critical to enforce our power plant emission controls to ensure that improvements in air quality for many are not at the expense of others' health.

Increasing the amount of clean energy in our electricity supply would improve air quality even further. Studies of the effect of plug-in cars on air quality tend to assume the status quo for our energy sources, leading to projections of high increases in the amount of coal supplying our electricity over the next few decades. Committing instead to get more of our electricity from clean sources such as wind and solar power would improve air quality significantly. And as discussed above, widespread use of electric cars will make it easier to increase the amount of clean energy in our grid, leading to decreases in air pollution from both cars and power plants.

| "Plug-in hybrid electric vehicles could cut U.S. gasoline use but could increase deadly air pollution in some areas."

Plug-in Electric Vehicles Will Increase Air Pollution

James R. Healey

While plug-in cars may reduce gasoline consumption in the United States, in some regions their use will actually result in increased air pollution, maintains James R. Healey in the following viewpoint. Since nearly half the electricity produced in the United States is generated using coal, low plug-in emissions will be offset by the pollution produced by the big power plants needed to create batteries for the plug-in cases. Even if plug-ins recharged using clean electricity, some studies show that plug-ins will generate more sulfur dioxide than gasoline or traditional hybrid vehicles, Healey asserts. Thus, he reasons, plug-ins are not completely clean. Healey has covered cars and the auto industry for USA Today *since January 1988.*

As you read, consider the following questions:

  1. According to Healey, what is true the longer a plug-in is designed to operate on just the batteries?

James R. Healey, "Plug-in Cars Could Actually Increase Air Pollution," *USA Today*, February 25, 2008. Reproduced by permission.

2. Why does the author say the Minnesota study numbers are striking?

3. What evidence does the author provide that the US Energy Department is backing plug-in hybrid vehicles?

The expected introduction of plug-in hybrid electric vehicles could cut U.S. gasoline use but could increase deadly air pollution in some areas, two reports say.

That's because a plug-in's lower tailpipe emissions may be offset by smokestack emissions from the utility generating plants supplying electricity to recharge the big batteries that allow plug-ins to run up to 40 miles without kicking on their gasoline engines. Plug-ins, called PHEVs, are partly powered, in effect, by the fuel used to generate the electricity.

Coal-Burning Vehicles

About 49% of U.S. electricity is generated using coal, so in some regions a plug-in running on its batteries is nearly the equivalent of a coal-burning vehicle. The trade-off is one that even plug-in backers acknowledge. It could undercut the appeal of vehicles that appear capable of using no gasoline in town and hitting 50 to 100 mpg [miles per gallon] overall fuel economy.

If large numbers of plug-in hybrids were being recharged with power from the least-sophisticated coal plants, "There is a possibility for significant increases of soot and mercury," says a report by environmental advocacy group Natural Resources Defense Council [NRDC]. Soot particles can make it hard to breathe, especially for asthmatics. Mercury is toxic.

"Plug-in hybrids are perhaps not good for all areas," says Howard Learner, executive director of the Environmental Law & Policy Center, a Chicago-based advocacy group. In "states that are heavily coal, that equation doesn't work out very well for the environment."

After PHEVs drain their stored energy, they operate like conventional hybrids, triggering their gasoline engines to help drive the wheels and recharge the batteries. Conventionals can't be plugged in; their batteries are recharged only while driving.

The longer a plug-in is designed to operate on just the batteries, the less gasoline it uses, but the more electricity it needs to recharge the larger batteries.

Thus, the better the PHEV—that is, the longer it goes just on its batteries—the greater the charge required and the more the pollution that might result from an electric utility's power generation.

Learner calls PHEVs "really important emerging technology—where the cleaner technologies are used to charge them."

Sulfur Dioxide Emissions

A study by the Minnesota Pollution Control Agency found plug-ins also could result in more sulfur dioxide (SO_2) emissions. SO_2 is toxic in large amounts and is a component of corrosive acid rain.

The Minnesota study found that use of PHEVs would lower most emissions compared with other vehicles, but that resulting SO_2 emissions would be more than double those from gasoline vehicles and about three or four times greater than from driving a regular hybrid. Exactly how much depends on how far the PHEV can run on battery power alone.

The Minnesota study also found that PHEVs would emit more carbon dioxide (CO_2) than driving a conventional hybrid. CO_2 is a greenhouse gas thought to contribute to global warming.

The Minnesota numbers are striking because they predict the big jump in SO_2 even if 40% of the state's electricity were generated by wind power, not coal or other polluting fuels. About 4% of the state's electricity now is from wind, according to state officials.

The state's PHEV study concludes: "Alternative vehicles offer benefits, but no single technology currently stands out as a clear choice."

The NRDC calculus shows that a plug-in charged from a power plant burning the dirtiest type of coal still has an overall pollution level less than a conventional gasoline car. But it would produce 11% more greenhouse gas emissions than a regular, non–plug-in hybrid, according to Luke Tonachel, vehicles analyst at the NRDC and co-author of the group's report on plug-ins. The report was produced jointly with the nonprofit Electric Power Research Institute.

He says, however, that charging a plug-in with electricity from renewable resources—wind or water, for instance—cuts overall greenhouse gas emissions to as low as a conventional gasoline car getting 74 mpg. No current gasoline car does that.

The NRDC and Minnesota studies were published last year [2007] but have yet to trigger alarms. PHEVs still are experimental; their possible threat is distant.

"It seems a little premature to think of it being a problem—but there are a lot of issues we should have been thinking of sooner," says Charles Griffith, auto project director at the Ecology Center, an environmental nonprofit based in Michigan. He cites as an example debate over use of land to grow crops for ethanol fuel vs. for food.

Even so, Griffith says, "The scenario where there are so many plug-in hybrids plugged into the (electric power) grid that you'll see a change in air quality just doesn't sound true to me."

On the Streets

Automakers say PHEVs could be on the streets in significant numbers within five years. Prototypes being tested by car companies suggest they should be able to go up to 40 miles on battery power, which could enable them to deliver average mileage in the neighborhood of 100 mpg in general driving.

The first plug-in vehicle in production, however, is likely to be General Motors' Chevrolet Volt, which is not a hybrid. Due in 2010 or 2011, Volt runs entirely on battery power. Like PHEVs, its battery pack can be recharged by plugging into a normal outlet, using electricity from a utility generating plant. A small gasoline engine recharges Volt's batteries when an outlet isn't handy, but unlike in a hybrid, that engine never directly powers the car. GM could sell 60,000 or more a year, forecasts consultant J.D. Power and Associates, if the price is $30,000 or less.

GM said at the Detroit auto show in January [2009] that it also will produce a plug-in hybrid version of its Saturn Vue SUV near the same time Volt is to launch.

Toyota Motor and Ford Motor each showed a prototype plug-in hybrid at auto shows this year and will test the designs. "It will come," says Toyota's Jaycie Chitwood, senior planner at the automaker's advanced technologies unit in the USA. "It's more a question of 'when' than 'if.'"

Ford's Greg Frenette, chief engineer of zero-emission vehicles, says it should take no more than five years to decide if plug-ins can be made reliable and inexpensive enough.

The U.S. Energy Department is backing PHEVs.

In January it offered $30 million for projects to "deliver up to 40 miles of electric range without recharging" and to make plug-ins "cost competitive by 2014 and ready for commercialization by 2016."

"We look at plug-in hybrids as the next generation of hybrids. They run cleaner, they save oil and they can save consumers money at the pump," NRDC's Tonachel says. But, he says, "Until our oldest power plants are replaced or upgraded, there could be increases in local particulate matter and ozone."

| *"Biofuels will play a role in a resilient, clean energy future."*

Biofuels Have the Potential to Reduce Polluting Greenhouse Gas Emissions

World Policy Institute

The World Policy Institute, a nonpartisan global policy think tank, claims in the following viewpoint that while biofuels involve social and environmental risks, these fuels are not as environmentally or economically destructive as some claim. Indeed, using new technologies and better land-use policies to refine biofuels will produce fewer greenhouse gases and reduce environmental degradation, the institute asserts. Moreover, the author maintains, the world's growing need for energy requires a more reasoned approach, in which the risks of biofuels are minimized and the benefits maximized.

As you read, consider the following questions:

1. What factors does the World Policy Institute argue make reliance on petroleum a risky proposition?

World Policy Institute, "Biofuels, Neither Savior nor Scam: The Case for a Selective Strategy," *World Policy Journal*, Spring 2008, pp. 9–13, 17. Copyright 2008 by Sage Publications Inc. Reproduced with permission of Sage Publications Inc. Journals.

2. According to the institute, what percentage of the growth in the global demand for liquid transport fuels has biofuels met?

3. According to recent articles cited by the author, what about the production of biofuels may lead to more, not less, greenhouse gas emissions?

Many people had never heard of biofuels two years ago [2006], yet now they are receiving a lot of publicity—much of it negative. Initially, political and business circles touted the potential benefits of biofuels; it was a speechwriter's dream. Here was an energy source that promised jobs, rural revitalization, and greater independence from foreign oil producers.

Concern About Climate Change

At a time of growing anxiety over global warming, biofuels promised a clean, liquid transport fuel that would help reduce levels of greenhouse gas emissions. According to the Intergovernmental Panel on Climate Change Fourth Assessment Report in early 2007, an estimated 1.8–4 degree Celsius rise in global temperatures is likely by the end of the century, if no dramatic change in energy supply and use occurs globally. The report further confirmed that, given the current state of scientific knowledge, it is 90 percent certain that the emissions caused by humans are responsible for the increasing warming of the planet's surface. Studies of climate patterns conclude with increased certainty that a continuing rise in greenhouse gas levels in the atmosphere will most likely result in a variety of alarming—and quite possibly catastrophic—climate impacts.

In European Union member states, Japan, and a number of other countries that have signed the Kyoto Protocol [an agreement by nations aimed at reducing greenhouse gases], concern about climate change has been a powerful policy driver for the biofuels industry. (Currently, transport fuels account for about a quarter of energy-related greenhouse gas emissions.)

The Promise of Biofuels

Meanwhile, with soaring gas prices and U.S. troops engaged in a war overseas, biofuels promised the added benefit of a secure, domestic energy source. The global transport system is almost entirely dependent on petroleum derivatives, and thus highly vulnerable. Leaving aside the complicated question of peak oil,[1] a number of factors increasingly make reliance on petroleum a risky proposition: petro-states such as Iran and Venezuela may threaten to cut production, continued conflict in the oil-rich Middle East may impede the flow of oil, and low global refining capacity creates dangerous bottlenecks in the current fuel system that leaves us susceptible to natural disasters and malicious attacks.

Add to this a moral component: The world is all but certain to struggle with the intertwined challenges of energy security and climate change, but it is humanity's poor who will suffer most, as they tend to live in regions most vulnerable to extreme weather events, often lack the means for secure shelter and transport, and are most affected by increased food prices and shrinking energy supplies. Globally, some 2.4 billion people rely on traditional biomass sources (firewood, oil, coal) for energy; and some 1.6 billion lack access to electricity. Without new energy solutions, 1.4 billion people will still lack electricity by 2030, the majority living in South Asia and sub-Saharan Africa. Some regions, notably the Caribbean, are almost completely dependent on imported petroleum for all of their energy needs. In these regions, even small amounts of domestically produced biofuels can help diversify fuel options, thereby reducing risk and vulnerability.

1. Peak oil refers to the point in the future when the rate at which oil can be pumped out of the ground peaks. Once that peak is reached, production rates will decline gradually over time.

With all these potential benefits, the biofuels market has grown by leaps and bounds over the past few years. There were some voices of caution during this giddy growth period, but they were largely unheeded. Just as popular sentiment had moved behind biofuels, it abruptly shifted course at an equally dizzying pace. The speed of the sea change in public opinion was shocking. Biofuels went from national savior to deadly scam in a matter of months. As wheat, corn, and rice prices reached new peaks this spring [2008], the food riots that spread through poorer countries in Asia, Africa, and the Caribbean have been increasingly linked in public debate to biofuels.

Neither a Panacea, nor a Scourge

Biofuels are neither a panacea nor a scourge. It is a valid concern that increased farming and production of biofuels are beginning to add pressure to stressed natural systems and failing social systems. It is clear that we need to develop energy alternatives, and quickly. The first and generally most cost-effective option is, and always should be, to reduce the consumption of petroleum through much more aggressive efficiency requirements, the development of lightweight materials for cars and trucks, improved battery technologies, new energy storage mechanisms, and the promotion of public transport. Biofuels belong within this portfolio of solutions. In total, biofuels today account for less than 2 percent of liquid transport fuels. This may seem like a small share, but biofuels have met about 30 percent of the growth in global demand for liquid transport fuels over the past three years. That is a significant contribution to the balance of the market.

In the European Union, for example, the 27 member states are currently required by law to meet volumetric biofuels targets. A target approved in 2003 stipulated that 5.75 percent of member states' fuel supplies must be composed of biofuels by 2010; this was followed in 2007 by a blending mandate calling

Biodiesel Reduces Emissions

Using 100 percent biodiesel (B100) eliminates all of the sulfur emissions associated with conventional diesel, cuts emissions of carbon monoxide and smog-producing particulate matter almost in half, and reduces hydrocarbon emissions by between 75 and 90 percent. Perhaps most significantly, using B100 reduces the emissions of carbon dioxide—the main greenhouse gas causing global warming—by more than 75 percent. Even using a blended biodiesel fuel like B20 (a 20 percent biodiesel/80 percent petrodiesel blend . . .) still reduces carbon dioxide emissions by 15 percent.

Andrew Korfhage, "The Benefits of Biodiesel,"
Green American, July–August 2006.

for renewable fuels to make up 10 percent of transport fuel supply by 2020. But if the member states revoke this requirement, as a growing chorus suggests—rather than attaching sustainability standards—they will have no influence over how biofuels are produced.

With biofuels, as with all energy resources, there are trade-offs and risks, but there are also opportunities. The challenge today is to deal rationally with this energy source by developing effective safeguards against the risks and capitalizing on the social and environmental opportunities.

Biofuel Sources

The two most common biofuels today are ethanol (made from starchy crops like sugarcane and corn) and biodiesel (which is generally derived from vegetable oils or animal fats). Ethanol is either blended with gasoline in low concentrations as an oxygenate or used at higher concentrations in flex-fuel vehicles (FFVs) that are designed to run on either unleaded gasoline or any blend of up to 85 percent ethanol. In the United States today, about half the gasoline sold at the pump is already 10 percent ethanol. Biodiesel can be used in diesel engines in either its pure form or as a blend with conventional diesel fuel. While these fuels hold significant potential to reduce greenhouse gas emissions and curb the global appetite for carbon-based petroleum products, there is now some concern over the emissions produced in the growing and refining of these fuels, as well as land-use issues, and their complex effect on food and grain prices.

But a second generation of advanced biofuels holds enormous potential to break through some of the key limitations of current fuels. Advanced biofuels (biobutanol and synthetic diesel, for example) and other biofuels derived from switchgrass, garbage, and algae are now under development in America, Europe, China, and elsewhere. Meanwhile, new conversion technologies are expected to expand production potential by allowing for the use of an array of nonfood biomass sources, which will greatly improve net greenhouse gas emissions and generate other positive environmental impacts.

Ethanol use, today's principal biofuel, has grown by some 12 percent annually over the past seven years, more than doubling its production. Still, biofuels currently account for less than 2 percent of global transport fuels and well below 1 percent of world agricultural land. Most ethanol is produced in the United States and Brazil, which together account for three-quarters of world output. In Brazil, ethanol comprises nearly 50 percent of the fuel at the pump. The United States produces more ethanol than Brazil, but total percentage at the pump domestically is still less than 5 percent, due to our massive fuel consumption. Biodiesel production has grown by 700 percent since 2000—largely in Europe—but total volume is still only about 10 percent of global ethanol production.

In the broader scope of global biomass utilization, liquid biofuels for transportation are but a tiny fraction of the whole. The majority of organic matter (or biomass) is used for animal feed, food, consumer goods, and building materials, with only a small percentage devoted specifically toward energy generation—and even less used to produce liquid biofuels. Still, there is considerable concern over the global rush to produce biofuels and it is critical to disaggregate the true issues from the din of the debate. . . .

The Greenhouse Gas Debate

One of the latest rounds in the biofuels debate centers on greenhouse gas emissions from indirect land-use changes. Currently, biofuels are made predominantly from food crops. But while biofuels account for a small fraction of total agricultural acreage, new fields and land are being cleared to produce biofuels and meet market demand. Increased cultivation adds pressure to already stressed ecosystems, requiring more land, water, and other natural resources. Perhaps the most urgent risk is the threat posed to native ecosystems, such as forests, that store massive amounts of carbon. In addition to disturbing wildlife, soils, and hydrological and nutrient cycles, the conversion of rain forest and native prairies to agricultural land releases enormous amounts of carbon—both from burning vegetation to clear fields and from tilling soil.

While current policy mechanisms are relatively efficacious in mitigating the direct impacts of biofuels production (for example, water pollution regulations on agricultural production in the United States would also apply to biofuels production), indirect impacts present a significant challenge, both to scientists and policy makers. Take one example: If American farmers begin to plant more corn for biofuels and less soy, it is likely that the global soy price will rise, creating added incentive for farmers in other parts of the world to increase soy production. Increased production can be achieved by increasing yields, expanding into new land, or substituting for other crops. The effects can be deleterious: increased pesticides and chemical inputs, wholesale clearing of land and native forests for biofuel feedstock cultivation, and crop displacement can dramatically increase greenhouse gas emissions. Thus, the calculus for assessing the indirect impact of, say, the growth in U.S. corn production for ethanol on global agriculture—and the associated greenhouse gas emissions—are enormously complex.

A Wide Range of Impacts

Recent articles in the authoritative journal on greenhouse gas emissions from land-use change caused indirectly from biofuels production have received wide attention. These articles have argued that virtually all biofuels produced today will result in more, not less, greenhouse gas emissions than the current use and production of fossil fuels. This has focused attention on a key issue, but it is important to realize that this field of research is very new—these studies are among the first ever peer-reviewed articles attempting to quantify greenhouse gas emissions impacts of indirect land-use changes. As such, many of the underlying assumptions are being questioned and the adequacy of the models and data sets used are being challenged. Numerous research efforts are under way around the world to better understand these land-use and greenhouse gas emission dynamics.

Thus, while biofuels offer significant potential for greenhouse gas emission reductions, there are risks. Even among current types of biofuels there exists a wide range in net emissions impacts. Some may indeed generate net increases in greenhouse gas emissions. Thus, it is critical that, as our understanding progresses, we begin to take a full life-cycle account of biofuel agriculture and production, including direct and indirect land-use changes, feedstock type, agricultural practices, energy replacement options, conversion and refining processes, and end use. Putting aside for a moment the potential greenhouse gas emissions from indirect land-use change, conventional corn-based ethanol is believed to produce roughly 15–35 percent net greenhouse gas emission reduction; soy-based biodiesel results in a net greenhouse gas emission reduction of 30–50 percent; cellulosic ethanol generates net greenhouse gas emissions reductions of 70–90 percent; and Brazilian sugarcane ethanol reduces net greenhouse emissions by 80–90 percent. These are considerable gains. . . .

A Role for Biofuels

Building a clean energy infrastructure, promoting greenhouse gas reductions, and ensuring plentiful and cheap food are daunting challenges, but they also present opportunities for new markets, new technologies, and new product development. Biofuels will play a role in a resilient, clean energy future, but we need smart policies and responsible, sustainable business practices.

The most egregious scare on the American people is not biofuels. Rather, it is the myopic debate that distracts from the larger issues at hand: Our current agricultural, energy, and transport systems are failing and putting us at risk by threatening the global climate. Human innovation, forward-thinking legislation, and collective action will be our saviors, not the fuel flavor of the day.

> "The enormous amounts of corn that
> ... ethanol processors buy from Mid-
> western farmers wreak damage on the
> environment in a multiplicity of ways."

Ethanol Increases Pollution

Sasha Lilley

*Hyped as an environmentally friendly fuel, ethanol actually in-
creases pollution, argues Sasha Lilley in the following viewpoint.
Although ethanol-based fuel is cleaner, ethanol processing plants,
which are powered by coal, emit greenhouse gases that contribute to global warming, she maintains. These processing plants
also generate sulfur dioxide, which contributes to respiratory illness and heart disease, Lilley claims. Moreover, she asserts, runoff from the fertilizer, herbicides, and insecticides used to grow
corn is polluting US waters. Unfortunately, Lilley concludes, the
companies that produce ethanol have the financial resources to
influence policy makers, making reasoned fuel policy difficult.
Lilley, who writes for CorpWatch, a corporate watchdog organization, produces the radio show* Against the Grain.

As you read, consider the following questions:

1. According to Mike Ewall, on what has the US Environmental Protection Agency cracked down in recent years?

Sasha Lilley, "The Dirty Truth About Green Fuel," *AlterNet*, June 7, 2006. Reproduced by permission of the author.

2. Despite the company's attempts at green packaging, why does Lilley dismiss the efforts of Archer Daniels Midland?

3. In the author's view, what hidden cost must be factored in to understand the true cost of producing corn-based ethanol?

The town of Columbus, Nebraska, bills itself as a "City of Power and Progress." If Archer Daniels Midland gets its way, that power will be partially generated by coal, one of the dirtiest forms of energy. When burned, it emits carcinogenic pollutants and high levels of the greenhouse gases linked to global warming.

Ironically this coal will be used to generate ethanol, a plant-based petroleum substitute that has been hyped by both environmentalists and President George Bush as the green fuel of the future. The agribusiness giant Archer Daniels Midland (ADM) is the largest U.S. producer of ethanol, which it makes by distilling corn. ADM also operates coal-fired plants at its company base in Decatur, Illinois, and Cedar Rapids, Iowa, and is currently adding another coal-powered facility at its Clinton, Iowa, ethanol plant.

Processing Plant Pollution

That's not all. "[Ethanol] plants themselves—not even the part producing the energy—produce a lot of air pollution," says Mike Ewall, director of the Energy Justice Network. "The EPA (U.S. Environmental Protection Agency) has cracked down in recent years on a lot of Midwestern ethanol plants for excessive levels of carbon monoxide, methanol, toluene, and volatile organic compounds, some of which are known to cause cancer."

A single ADM corn processing plant in Clinton, Iowa, generated nearly 20,000 tons of pollutants including sulfur dioxide, nitrogen oxides, and volatile organic compounds in 2004, according to federal records. The EPA considers an ethanol plant as a "major source" of pollution if it produces more than 100 tons of any one pollutant per year, although it has recently proposed increasing that cap to 250 tons.

Sulfur dioxide is classified by the EPA as a contributor to respiratory and heart disease and the generation of acid rain. Nitrogen oxides produce ozone and a wide variety of toxic chemicals as well as contributing to global warming, according to the EPA, while many volatile organic compounds are cancer causing. Last year [2005], Environmental Defense [currently known as Environmental Defense Fund], a national environmental group, ranked the Clinton plant as the 26th largest emitter of carcinogenic compounds in the U.S.

For years, ADM promoted itself as the "supermarket to the world" on major U.S. radio and television networks like NPR, CBS, NBC, and PBS where it underwrites influential programs such as the *NewsHour with Jim Lehrer*. Now, as it actively promotes its ethanol business, ADM has rolled out its new eco-friendly slogan, "Resourceful by Nature," which "reinforces our role as an essential link between farmers and consumers."

Despite the company's attempts at green packaging, ADM is ranked as the tenth worst corporate air polluter on the "Toxic 100" list of the Political Economy Research Institute at the University of Massachusetts. The Department of Justice and the Environmental Protection Agency have charged the company with violations of the Clean Air Act in hundreds of processing units, covering 52 plants in 16 states. In 2003 the two agencies reached a $351 million settlement with the company. Three years earlier, ADM was fined $1.5 million by the Department of Justice and $1.1 million by the state of Illinois for pollution related to ethanol production and distribution. Currently, the corporation is involved in approximately 25 administrative and judicial proceedings connected to federal and state Superfund laws [referring to regulations under the Comprehensive Environmental Response, Compensation, and Liability Act] regarding the environmental cleanup of sites contaminated by ADM operations.

Friends in High Places

Environmentalists have cried foul, but they are up against the 56th largest company in the United States, as ranked by revenue in *Fortune* magazine. ADM has more than 25,000 employees, net sales last year of $35.9 billion, with $1 billion in profits, as well as a recent 29 percent profit increase in the last quarter. The company is a global force: ADM is one of the world's biggest processors of soybeans, corn, wheat, and cocoa, which it buys from growers in the U.S. and around the world. The company recently hired Patricia A. Woertz, an executive vice president of Chevron Corporation, as its chief executive officer.

ADM has another resource at its disposal, the considerable clout it has built up over decades of courting and lobbying Washington's power brokers. Days after the company's February [2006] expansion announcement of the coal-fired Nebraska plant, U.S. Energy Secretary Samuel W. Bodman visited ADM's Decatur headquarters to tout its part in President Bush's biofuels initiative. The secretary posed for photos with then ADM Chair G. Allen Andreas and announced that the Department of Energy would offer up to $160 million for the construction of three biorefineries to expand U.S. ethanol production.

"Partnerships with industries like these will lead to new innovation and discovery that will usher in an era of reduced dependence on foreign sources of oil, while strengthening our economy at home," Secretary Bodman said from ADM's trade floor. Like the ADM ethanol plant in Columbus, the three biorefineries could well be partially coal-powered, given the absence of conditions imposed by the Department of Energy.

"It's been some 30 years since we got a call from the White House asking for the agricultural industry, ADM in particular,

Problems with Corn Ethanol

Not only does ethanol not reduce the emission of greenhouse gases, ethanol burning contributes notable amounts of atmospheric nitrogen oxides, which then combine with volatile organic compounds (VOCs) to produce ozone. Studies show conclusively that ethanol leads to an increased ozone problem. Within half a year of switching entirely to ethanol additives, California ozone levels rose 22%, and exceedances of the 8-hour standard rose to a maximum concentration of 40%.

Ethanol plants are also notorious polluters, emitting ethanol vapors, carbon monoxide, VOCs, and carcinogens. In the last few years, the EPA [Environmetal Protection Agency] has had to crack down on ethanol plants discharging 5 to 430 times more VOCs and carcinogens than their permits allow. The EPA has stated that the problem is common to most, if not all, ethanol plants. As of 2002, there were 61 ethanol plants in the US, located mostly in the Midwest, with another 14 under construction.

Dale Allen Pfeiffer, "The Dirty Truth About Biofuels,"
Mountain Sentinel, April 11, 2006.

to take a serious look at the possibilities of building facilities to produce alternative sources of energy for our fuel supply in the United States," said [G.] Allen Andreas, who was chair, chief executive and president of ADM at the time of Secretary Bodman's visit. "We are delighted to participate in any way that we can in the president's programs."

Cultivating Support

ADM and its signature project have never lacked friends in high places, despite a history of price-fixing scandals and monopolistic misdeeds. The Andreas family, which has headed up the publicly traded company for decades, has cultivated bipartisan support through generous donations to both Republicans and Democrats. Since the 2000 election cycle, ADM has given more than $3 million in political contributions, according to the Center for Responsive Politics: $1.2 million to Democrats and $1.85 million to Republicans. These donations may have helped sustain a multitude of government subsidies to ADM, including ethanol tax credits, tariffs against foreign ethanol competitors, and federally mandated ethanol additive standards.

Politicians from the Midwestern Corn Belt are some of the company's staunchest allies. Senators Richard Durbin, Charles Grassley, and Tom Harkin, and Representative Dick Gephardt have consistently supported lavish federal tax subsidies to ethanol producers, for which ADM is the prime beneficiary. All are recipients of political action committee donations from the agribusiness behemoth. The *Wall Street Journal* has referred to the former South Dakota senator and Senate minority leader [Tom Daschle] as "Archer Daschle Midland," because of his unswerving support for the interests of the company.

ADM's political heft was behind the 54 cent per gallon tariff that the U.S. government has imposed on imports of sugarcane-based ethanol from Brazil, which is cheaper than ADM's corn-based fuel. The tariff dates back to 1980 when the CEO of ADM convinced President [Jimmy] Carter to adopt it, according to former ADM lobbyist Joseph Karth. Iowa's Senator Grassley recently stated his intention to block any attempt to remove the tariff on lower-cost Brazilian fuel in the face of rising gas prices, stating that "lifting this tariff would be counterproductive to the widely supported goal of promoting homegrown renewable sources of energy."

Government Largesse

Over many decades, the company has been the recipient of government largesse in the form of federal and state corn and ethanol subsidies that have totaled billions of dollars, prompting the libertarian Cato Institute to declare ADM the biggest recipient of corporate welfare in the U.S. in 1995. ADM has been a prime beneficiary of the federal tax credit on ethanol, which the refiner can apply to the tax it pays on corporate income. First implemented in 1978, the tax credit currently stands at 51 cents per gallon of ethanol sold. The Government Accounting Office [currently known as the Government Accountability Office] estimates the subsidies to the ethanol industry from 1980–2000 at $11 billion. As the biggest ethanol producer in the U.S., ADM has received the largest portion of the government's generosity.

Recent legislation has further greased the tracks of the ethanol gravy train. The Energy Policy Act of 2005's Renewable Fuel Standard stipulates that gasoline sold in the U.S. must include a certain percentage of ethanol or biodiesel, starting at 4 billion gallons this year and rising to 7.5 billion gallons by 2012. ADM got another boost when the federal government mandated that oil companies replace MTBE, a cancer-causing gasoline additive, with ethanol. 45 states have adopted policies to encourage the production and use of the fuel. ADM has responded with plans to increase its output of ethanol by 42 percent over the next three years.

When Corn Is King

Subsidies and tax incentives might make public policy sense—even when they flow into the coffers of a Fortune 500 company with mega-profits—but only if corn ethanol delivers on the promise that its boosters claim: to significantly cut greenhouse emissions, protect the environment, and slow global warming.

Debate has raged for years over whether ethanol made from corn generates more energy than the amount of fossil fuel that is used to produce it. UC [University of California] Berkeley's Alexander Farrell recently co-authored a comprehensive study, published in *Science*, on the energy and greenhouse gas output of various sources of ethanol. His group found that corn ethanol reduces greenhouse gases by only 13 percent, which compares unfavorably with ethanol made from vegetable cellulose such as switchgrass. "Our best guess," says Farrell, "is that using corn ethanol today results in a modest decline of greenhouse gas emissions."

Yet the enormous amounts of corn that ADM and other ethanol processors buy from Midwestern farmers wreak damage on the environment in a multiplicity of ways. Modern corn hybrids require more nitrogen fertilizer, herbicides, and insecticides than any other crop, while causing the most extensive erosion of top soil. Pesticide and fertilizer runoff from the vast expanses of corn in the U.S. prairies bleed into groundwater and rivers as far as the Gulf of Mexico. The nitrogen runoff flowing into the Mississippi River has fostered a vast bloom of dead algae in the Gulf that starves fish and other aquatic life of oxygen.

The Hidden Costs

To understand the hidden costs of corn-based ethanol requires factoring in "the huge, monstrous costs of cleaning up polluted water in the Mississippi River drainage basin and also trying to remedy the negative effects of poisoning the Gulf of Mexico," says Tad Patzek of the University of California's Civil and Environmental Engineering department.

"These are not abstract environmental effects," Patzek asserts, "these are effects that impact the drinking water all over the Corn Belt, that impact also the poison that people ingest when they eat their food, from the various pesticides and herbicides." Corn farming substantially tops all crops in total application of pesticides, according to the U.S. Department of Agriculture, and is the crop most likely to leach pesticides into drinking water.

While banned by the European Union, atrazine is the most heavily used herbicide in the United States—primarily applied to cornfields—and the EPA rates it as the second most common pesticide in drinking wells. The EPA has set maximum safe levels of atrazine in drinking water at 3 parts per billion, but scientists with the U.S. Geological Survey have found up to 224 parts per billion in Midwestern streams and 2,300 parts per billion in Corn Belt irrigation reservoirs.

Then there is the question of how practical it is to replace petroleum with corn-based ethanol. "There are conflicting figures on how much land would be needed to meet all of our petroleum demand from ethanol," says Energy Justice Network's Ewall, "and those range from some portion of what we currently have as available crop land to as much as five times as the amount of crop land in the U.S." The Department of Agriculture estimates that the Corn Belt has lost 90 percent of its original wetlands, two thirds of which has taken place since draining for agriculture began mid-century.

"No one who's looked at this issue [from an environmental perspective] talks about using corn kernels as the only, or even major component, of the long-term solution," counters Nathanael Greene, senior policy analyst with the Natural Resources Defense Council. "Everyone assumes we'll evolve the industry from its current technology to the advanced technologies."

If that happens, it will be a marked reversal of many decades of government policy in support of Archer Daniels Midland—and the company may well wonder what it's getting for its unceasingly ample gifts to both political parties. But with the "full-throated support of the Bush administration," in the words of the Renewable Fuels Association, a corn ethanol-dominated, ADM-led trade group, that day doesn't seem to be approaching any time soon.

> *"By using nuclear energy rather than fossil fuel-based plants, electric utilities prevented 647 million metric tons of carbon dioxide emissions in the United States in 2009."*

Nuclear Power Will Reduce Air Pollution

Nuclear Energy Institute

In the following viewpoint, the Nuclear Energy Institute (NEI) maintains that nuclear power will reduce pollution. Indeed, the institute asserts, each year nuclear energy prevents the emission of more than 2 billion metric tons of the carbon dioxide that contributes to global warming. Nuclear power does emit some greenhouse gases over the period of its entire life cycle, but studies show that these life cycle emissions are similar to solar, wind, and hydropower, the institute claims. Thus, NEI reasons, policy makers recognize that nuclear energy has a role to play in greenhouse gas reduction policies. NEI promotes the beneficial uses of nuclear energies and technologies worldwide.

Nuclear Energy Institute, "Nuclear Energy Plays Essential Role in Climate Change Initiatives," www.nei.org, August 2010. Reprinted by permission. Some of the material summarized in this book is the property of the Nuclear Energy Institute (NEI). Copyright © 2010 by NEI. That material has been used and reprinted here with permission from NEI. NEI does not warrant the accuracy or completeness of the summary of its material, and disclaims any and all liability stemming from any uses of or reliance upon the material. No NEI material may be copied or reprinted without NEI's permission.

As you read, consider the following questions:

1. The volume of greenhouse gas emissions prevented at nuclear power plants is equivalent to what percentage of reduction, according to NEI?

2. According to the author, if all existing US nuclear power plants retire, how many new plants must be built by 2050?

3. Other than carbon-free energy, what other benefits are there to increasing America's reliance on nuclear energy?

Key Points

- The nuclear energy industry supports the administration's goal of transitioning the United States to a clean energy, low-carbon economy. According to independent analyses, a significant expansion of nuclear energy is essential to meet this goal.

- In 2009, the Nuclear Energy Institute proposed a comprehensive package of policy initiatives to facilitate the expansion of nuclear energy in coming decades on the scale that independent analyses conclude is required to ensure a reliable supply of low-carbon electricity. . . .

- Nuclear energy has played a major role in reducing U.S. emissions of carbon dioxide, sulfur dioxide and nitrogen oxides by substituting for fossil fuels that otherwise would have been burned to generate electricity. The 104 U.S. nuclear power plants operating in 31 states provide electricity for one in five homes and businesses without emitting carbon dioxide, the major greenhouse gas. In fact, nuclear energy provides almost 70 percent of the electricity that comes from emission-free sources, which also include renewable technologies and hydroelectric power plants.

- Nuclear energy is the only scalable option available today that can provide base load electricity production
  24/7 economically and without emitting greenhouse
  gases. Even if carbon dioxide emissions are evaluated
  on a total life cycle basis, nuclear energy is comparable
  to renewable energy sources such as solar, wind and
  hydropower.

Nuclear Energy's Vital Role in Reducing Greenhouse Gas Emissions

Carbon dioxide—a significant greenhouse gas emitted by human activity—is the major focus of policy discussions to
combat climate change. At a time when the United States faces
a projected 28 percent increase in electricity demand by 2035,
failure to develop a holistic policy that meets the nation's energy demands, security needs and greenhouse gas reduction
goals could threaten progress toward these objectives.

According to the Environmental Protection Agency, the
largest source of carbon dioxide emissions globally is the
combustion of fossil fuels (coal, oil and natural gas) in power
plants, automobiles, industrial facilities and other sources.
Generating electricity is the single largest source of carbon dioxide emissions, representing 41 percent of all emissions.

Nuclear power plants produce electricity without emitting
carbon dioxide or other greenhouse gases. Nuclear energy
provides about one-fifth of U.S. electricity—and almost 70
percent of the nation's carbon-free electricity.

Globally, 441 nuclear reactors generate about 14 percent of
the world's electricity. Construction is under way on 61 reactors, and 149 reactors are on order or planned in 29 countries.
More than 500 reactors are under consideration worldwide,
according to the World Nuclear Association.[1]

1. "World Nuclear Power Reactors & Uranium Requirements," World Nuclear Association, Aug. 1, 2010.

Nuclear power plants already play a powerful role in preventing greenhouse gases in the electricity sector. By using nuclear energy rather than fossil fuel-based plants, electric utilities prevented 647 million metric tons of carbon dioxide emissions in the United States in 2009. For perspective, the volume of greenhouse gas emissions prevented at nuclear power plants is equivalent to taking 92 percent of all passenger cars off America's roadways. In the near future, nuclear energy could help decarbonize the transportation sector by providing carbon-free electricity to plug-in hybrid electric vehicles and electric light rail.

Worldwide, nuclear energy prevents the emission of more than 2.6 billion metric tons of carbon dioxide each year.

Diverse Groups Recognize Nuclear Energy's Climate-Friendly Benefits

U.S. policy makers are weighing legislative and other approaches for reducing greenhouse gas emissions. While many predict that meaningful climate change policy may take several years to finalize, the role that nuclear energy can play in carbon reduction programs is clear. All mainstream analyses of the climate change issue by independent organizations show that reducing carbon emissions will require a portfolio of technologies, that nuclear energy must be part of the portfolio, and that major expansion of nuclear generating capacity over the next few decades is essential.

The Obama administration has made energy legislation a priority, and the U.S. Congress continues to debate climate change legislation. In 2009, the House of Representatives approved the American Clean Energy and Security Act (H.R. 2454). The bill's primary goal is reducing carbon emissions by 83 percent by 2050.

Analyses of H.R. 2454 by EPA and the U.S. Energy Information Administration (EIA) demonstrate that substantial increases in nuclear generating capacity will be essential to meet the legislation's carbon-reduction goals.

In the EPA analysis, nuclear generation increases by 150 percent, from 782 billion kilowatt-hours (kWh) in 2005 to 2,081 billion kWh in 2050. If all existing U.S. nuclear power plants retire after 60 years of operation, 181 new nuclear plants must be built by 2050.

In the "Basic" scenario in the EIA's analysis, the United States would need to build 96 gigawatts of new nuclear generation by 2030 (roughly 69 new nuclear plants). This would result in nuclear energy supplying 33 percent of U.S. electricity generation, more than any other source of electric power. According to the analysis, to the extent the United States cannot deploy new nuclear power plants in these numbers, the cost of electricity, natural gas and carbon allowances will be higher.

In September 2009, Sens. John Kerry (D-Mass.) and Barbara Boxer (D-Calif.) introduced the Clean Energy Jobs and American Power Act (S. 1733), which aims to create clean-energy jobs, reduce greenhouse gases and enhance domestic energy protection. The bill states, "It is the policy of the United States . . . to facilitate the continued development and growth of a safe and clean nuclear energy industry."

Several other bills that address energy and climate change have been introduced in the Senate.

In June 2010, Sen. Richard Lugar (R-Ind.) introduced the Practical Energy and Climate Plan (S. 3464). Sens. Lindsey Graham (R-S.C.) and Lisa Murkowski (R-Alaska) co-sponsored the bill. The legislation is an alternative to the cap-and-trade approach that seeks to "establish a future for cleaner coal usage, boost nuclear power, enhance deployment of diverse renewable power sources, and cut overall energy demand growth through efficiency."

Also in June 2010, Sens. Richard Burr (R-N.C.) and Saxby Chambliss (R-Ga.) introduced a bill to expand America's use of cleaner, domestic energy resources. The Next Generation Energy Security Act (S. 3535) envisions the use of natural gas vehicles and the expansion of nuclear energy and includes measures to encourage used nuclear fuel recycling and the use of renewables.

In July 2010, Sen. George Voinovich (R-Ohio) introduced the Enabling the Nuclear Renaissance Act (S. 3618), which gathers into a single bill many nuclear energy provisions found in previously introduced legislation. Sen. Voinovich's legislation proposed establishing several offices within DOE [U.S. department of Energy] to handle nuclear energy issues and a new government corporation—Fed Corp—to assume responsibility from DOE for implementing the disposition of used nuclear fuel.

Analyses See Important Role for Nuclear Energy

Analyses and reports from other organizations recognize nuclear energy's potential in mitigating climate change, including:

- An Environmental Protection Agency analysis of the American Power Act of 2010 (Kerry/Lieberman). The report's core policy scenario for reducing greenhouse gas emissions would require more than doubling total nuclear capacity by 2050, the equivalent of building 181 new reactors.

- A study from the United Nations Framework Convention on Climate Change that called for an additional investment by utilities of $25 billion in nuclear energy by 2030.

- The World Economic Forum's 2008 analysis of energy stated that nuclear energy is "probably the best option for carbon-neutral energy from the perspective of currently available and easily scalable technologies." In

2009, the forum's Task Force on Low-Carbon Prosperity recommended establishing a platform for an international public-private dialogue "to discuss the role of nuclear power in the low-carbon economy and how the related policy architecture should be designed to reflect its contribution."

- A joint statement from the academies of science of the G8+5 [leaders from the Group of Eight plus the leaders from five developing nations] countries recommended accelerating the transition to a "low carbon economy" by producing more energy from low-carbon sources such as nuclear power.

- The "Prism/MERGE Analyses: 2009 Update" from the Electric Power Research Institute, which concluded that 45 new reactors are needed to reduce carbon dioxide levels by 41 percent from 2005 levels by 2030.

- The 2009 "World Energy Outlook" report from the International Energy Agency concluded that stabilizing atmospheric concentrations of carbon dioxide at 450 parts per million would require nearly doubling global nuclear energy capacity by 2030. . . .

Federal Policies Needed to Support Nuclear Energy's Expansion

A major expansion of nuclear energy generation requires federal policy in a number of areas, including:

- new plant financing, principally through creation of a Clean Energy Deployment Administration that would function as a permanent financing platform

- tax incentives for nuclear energy manufacturing and production facilities and workforce development

- ensuring achievement of the efficiencies in the new plant licensing process that was established in 1992, but is only now being tested

- management of used nuclear fuel, including limited financial incentives for the development of voluntary interim storage facilities for used uranium fuel and re-search and development on recycling technology

- nuclear fuel supply, to enhance the certainty and trans-parency associated with the disposition of government inventories on uranium markets

- other areas, such as creation of a National Nuclear Energy Council to advise the secretary of energy and authorization of a federal program to advance development and deployment of small modular reactors within the next 15 years.

NEI has developed proposed legislation to address these issues. Details on NEI's 2009 policy initiative are available at http://www.nei.org/resourcesandstats/documentlibrary/new plants/policybrief/2009-nuclear-policy-initiative.

Increasing America's reliance on nuclear energy will serve other national imperatives besides the production of carbon-free electricity. Construction of new nuclear power plants will create tens of thousands of jobs—to build the plants and to produce the components and materials that go into the plants. A nuclear construction program also will breathe new life into the U.S. manufacturing sector, as it rebuilds and retools to produce the necessary pumps, valves, reactor vessels and other nuclear-grade equipment needed for new nuclear plants.

Analyses Recommending an Expanded Role for Nuclear Energy

- Environmental Protection Agency, "EPA Analysis of the American Power Act of 2010 (Kerry/Lieberman)," June

2010: The core policy scenario for reducing greenhouse gas emissions would require more than doubling total nuclear capacity by 2050. If all existing U.S. operating reactors retire at 60 years, the U.S. will need to build another 253 gigawatts of nuclear capacity (approximately 181 new reactors).

- Environmental Protection Agency, "EPA Analysis of the American Clean Energy and Security Act of 2009 (H.R. 2454)," June 2009: The core policy scenario for reducing greenhouse gas emissions would require a 150 percent increase in nuclear power generation, or roughly 180 new reactors, by 2050.

- Joint Statement of the Academies of Science for the G8+5 Countries, "Climate Change Adaptation and the Transition to a Low Carbon [Society]," 2008: The statement recommends accelerating the transition to a low-carbon economy by producing more energy from low-carbon sources such as nuclear power.

- Electric Power Research Institute, "Prism/MERGE Analyses: 2009 Update": Full portfolio approach to reducing carbon dioxide emissions by 41 percent from 2005 levels by 2030 includes 45 new nuclear reactors.

- U.S. Energy Information Administration, "Energy Market and Economic Impacts of H.R. 2454, the American Clean Energy and Security Act of 2009," August 2009: The basic scenario projects that the United States would need 96 gigawatts of new nuclear capacity, almost 70 new reactors, by 2030.

- OECD [Organisation for Economic Co-operation and Development]/International Energy Agency, "World Energy Outlook 2009," OECD/IEA, 2009: Stabilizing atmospheric concentrations of carbon dioxide at 450 parts per million would require nearly doubling global nuclear energy capacity by 2030.

- Business Roundtable, "The Balancing Act: Climate Change, Energy Security and the U.S. Economy," 2009: "As the only existing, proven and scalable low-carbon base load generation technology, nuclear power will be critical to managing the impending turnover in base load capacity in a sustainable manner."

> *"A major national investment in nuclear power would actually set America back in its efforts to reduce pollution."*

Nuclear Power Will Hinder Efforts to Reduce Air Pollution

Travis Madsen, Tony Dutzik, Bernadette Del Chiaro, and Rob Sargent

The authors of the following viewpoint maintain that nuclear power will hinder pollution reduction efforts. Building safe, efficient nuclear reactors takes time; thus these reactors would not be running in time to meet greenhouse gas reduction targets, the authors assert. In addition, they argue, spending current energy funds on nuclear power plants diverts money from clean energy solutions that would reduce global warming pollution almost immediately. In fact, the authors claim, investing in clean energy now could double the impact of investment in nuclear power. Madsen and Dutzik represent the Frontier Group, and Del Chiaro and Sargent represent Environment America Research & Policy Center.

Travis Madsen, Tony Dutzik, Bernadette Del Chiaro, and Rob Sargent, "Generating Failure: How Building Nuclear Power Plants Would Set America Back in the Race Against Global Warming," Environment America Research and Policy Center and Frontier Group, November 2009. Reproduced by permission.

As you read, consider the following questions:

1. In the authors' opinion, if construction follows historical patterns, when would the next new nuclear reactor be up and running?

2. According to the authors, how long would it take to build a utility scale wind farm?

3. In the authors' view, should the highest cost forecasts come true, how much might building one hundred new nuclear reactors cost?

Nuclear power is not necessary to provide reliable, low-carbon electricity for the future. Far from being a solution to global warming, a major national investment in nuclear power would actually set America back in its efforts to reduce pollution. Even building 100 nuclear reactors by 2030 would be too slow to make enough of a difference, and too expensive compared to other sources of clean, emission-free electricity. And that investment—which would likely run into the trillions of dollars—would foreclose opportunities to invest in other clean technologies with the potential to deliver greater emission reductions, faster.

Nuclear Power Is Too Slow

Building 100 new nuclear reactors would happen too slowly to reduce global warming pollution in the near term, and would actually increase the scale of emission cuts required in the future.

At best, the nuclear industry could have a new reactor up and running by 2016, assuming that construction could be completed in four years. This pace would be faster than 80 to 95 percent of all reactors completed during the last wave of reactor construction in the United States. If construction follows historical patterns, it could take nine years after a license is issued before the first reactor is up and running—into the 2020s.

Under this very plausible scenario, new nuclear power could make no contribution toward reducing U.S. emissions of global warming pollution by 2020—despite the investment of hundreds of billions of dollars for the construction of nuclear power plants. And even if the industry completed 100 new reactors by 2030, which is highly unlikely, these reactors would reduce cumulative power plant emissions of carbon dioxide over the next two decades by only 12 percent below business as usual, when a reduction of more than 70 percent is called for. In other words, 100 new nuclear reactors would be too little, too late to successfully meet our goals for limiting the severity of global warming. . . .

Clean Energy Solutions Can Reduce Pollution Faster

Clean energy solutions have a significant advantage over nuclear power when it comes to reducing global warming pollution. Individual clean energy measures are small—as simple as installing a new lightbulb in a home or erecting a single wind turbine. Small means fast. Millions of individual workers could participate in a clean energy transition at the same time. And many individual clean energy measures can add up to a rapid, large-scale cut in emissions. . . .

Individual energy efficiency and clean energy measures can be implemented in a matter of minutes to just a few years. Each individual measure delivers results right away. For example:

- Designing and building a super energy-efficient building requires little to no extra time compared to the effort required to build and design a standard building. Simple changes in design and construction can yield homes, institutions, and commercial buildings that use 70 percent less energy than standard structures. Adding small-scale clean energy systems—solar photovoltaic panels or small wind turbines, for instance—can yield buildings that produce as much energy as they consume over the course of an entire year.

- Retrofitting an existing structure to achieve higher energy performance can take a matter of days to months to a few years. Contractors can weatherize an existing home in an average of three days. Installing a home solar photovoltaic system typically takes less than a week. Larger businesses or institutions can upgrade lighting, heating and cooling equipment, or mechanical systems in a matter of months to just a few years.

- With available transmission infrastructure, today's power companies can build a utility-scale wind farm in as little as one year, and a concentrating solar thermal power plant in as little as two to three years after groundbreaking. The components of these systems are largely modular. Making a bigger wind farm simply requires installing more wind turbines, and making a larger solar power plant basically requires installing more mirrors or more steam turbines. The modular and scalable nature of construction makes projects simple relative to traditional coal-fired or nuclear power plants, and better able to take advantage of economies of scale. Wind, concentrating solar thermal, and geothermal energy, however, must be integrated into the transmission grid. Projects that require major new power lines to be built could take longer to complete.

- Production of large amounts of energy-efficient products and renewable energy technologies can be ramped up quickly. For example, worldwide capacity for solar panel production nearly doubled in 2008 alone and has increased by roughly fivefold since 2004.

Adding Up to Substantial Results

Clean energy measures are individually small and modular, but massed together, they can deliver substantial emissions reductions within just a few years.

- Energy efficiency programs active now in states such as California, Oregon, Connecticut, Vermont and New York are supplying most new electricity needs—cutting electricity consumption by 1–2 percent below forecast levels per year. Reducing electricity consumption by 1.2 percent per year (below a no additional action forecast) across America as a whole, starting in 2010, could deliver the same amount of energy as building more than 30 nuclear reactors by 2016—the earliest possible date the U.S. could have even three new reactors up and running.

- In 2008, the wind industry brought 8,500 MW [megawatts] of wind energy generation capacity online, with another 4,000 MW in the first half of 2009. The installations increased U.S. wind energy capacity by more than 50 percent—two years ahead of schedule on a trajectory to supply 20 percent of America's electricity by 2030, as mapped out by the U.S. Department of Energy. Wind accounted for almost half of all new generation capacity completed in 2008. In energy equivalent terms, these new wind turbines are equal to more than three new nuclear reactors. Wind energy experts predict that wind will become the dominant source of new electric generating capacity in 2009–2012, with 36,000 to 40,000 MW installed (the energy equivalent of 10–12 new nuclear reactors).

- The concentrating solar power industry is actively installing facilities in the southwestern United States, with 8,500 MW of generating capacity expected to be online

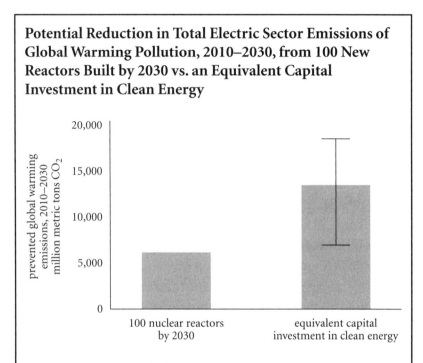

Potential Reduction in Total Electric Sector Emissions of Global Warming Pollution, 2010–2030, from 100 New Reactors Built by 2030 vs. an Equivalent Capital Investment in Clean Energy

TAKEN FROM: Travis Madsen, Tony Dutzik, Bernadette Del Chiaro, and Rob Sargent, "Generating Failure: How Building Nuclear Power Plants Would Set America Back in the Race Against Global Warming," Environment America, November 2009.

by 2014. This capacity is the rough energy equivalent of two to three nuclear reactors. Rooftop solar photovoltaic panels are booming as well, with California alone on pace to install 3,000 MW by 2017.

Doubling the Impact

Through 2030, investing in clean energy could deliver double the impact of a comparable investment in nuclear power. The speed at which small, modular clean energy measures can be deployed means that capital invested in clean energy can begin preventing pollution right away, making a bigger overall difference in the next two decades.

Cost estimates for new nuclear reactors vary widely, since none have been built in the U.S. in more than 30 years. The U.S. Department of Energy has put forward one of the most optimistic forecasts of possible nuclear reactor costs over the next two decades, projecting that the capital cost of reactor construction could be as low as $2,400 per kilowatt (kW) by 2030 (in 2007 dollars). (Many independent experts find this estimate implausible.) However, even if building a nuclear reactor turns out to be this inexpensive and quick, 100 new nuclear reactors by 2030 could—at best—prevent the same amount of pollution as investing that same capital into clean energy solutions such as energy efficiency.

On the other hand, if building a new nuclear reactor turns out to be an expensive and time-consuming endeavor, like many reactors built in the 1970s, reactors could cost as much as $10,000 per kW (2008 dollars). Putting that level of capital investment into energy efficiency and renewable energy technologies instead would prevent three times as much pollution by 2030.

At a mid-range reactor cost estimate of $6,250 per kW (2008 dollars), putting an equivalent investment into energy efficiency and renewable energy would prevent twice as much pollution by 2030 as building 100 new reactors. . . .

Diverting Resources from More Cost-Effective Strategies

Choosing to build new reactors would divert resources from more cost-effective strategies. Building 100 new nuclear reactors could have an up-front cost on the order of $600 billion (with a possible range of $250 billion to $1 trillion). Investing this money in reactor deployment would foreclose opportunities to pursue cheaper and faster options.

New nuclear reactors would be far more costly than other forms of emission-free electricity. Even the most optimistic estimates for the average cost of power from a new nuclear reactor are 300 percent higher than the cost of energy efficiency or the cost of co-firing biomass in an existing power plant, and well above renewable technologies like wind power. Moreover, any new nuclear reactors won't be operational until well into the next decade, whereas clean energy sources can be deployed now.

The cost advantages that clean energy has over nuclear power are likely to become even more pronounced over time, while we wait for the nuclear industry to finish its first new reactor. According to Moody's Investor Service, ". . . nuclear generation has a fixed design where construction costs are rising rapidly, while other renewable technologies are still experiencing significant advancements in terms of energy conversion efficiency and cost reductions." . . .

What Could an Equivalent Capital Investment in Clean Energy Achieve?

Investing $600 billion could potentially get us 100 new nuclear reactors by 2030. Alternatively, if we invested that money in clean energy solutions, we could get double the impact, without the drag on the economy that the high cost of nuclear power would impose.

At an optimistic reactor cost forecast used by the Energy Information Administration of around $2,500 per kW of capacity, building 100 new reactors would cost $250 billion up front. Investing that same amount of capital in energy efficiency could reduce America's electricity consumption by about 12 percent below the reference case by 2030. This level of investment in energy efficiency would deliver emission reductions equal to building 100 new nuclear reactors by 2030, but unlike nuclear, pollution prevented through efficiency would come at net savings, since energy efficiency is so much more cost effective than building new reactors.

At mid-range costs of around $6,500 per kW, near those forecast by Moody's and comparable to recently proposed reactors, building 100 nuclear reactors would cost $650 billion. Directing $590 billion of this capital investment to efficiency measures could capture a large fraction of America's identified potential for electric energy efficiency, reducing electricity consumption by 25 percent below business as usual by 2030. The remaining money could purchase enough wind turbines and other renewable energy equipment to generate an additional 130 billion kWh by 2030. Altogether, this package of clean energy would yield as much energy as more than 170 nuclear reactors in 2030. This package of clean energy would reduce twice as much pollution as nuclear through 2030, with net savings on electricity costs—which nuclear power cannot offer.

Should the highest cost forecasts for nuclear power come true, building 100 new reactors could cost $1 trillion. This level of investment in clean energy solutions could yield as much electricity as more than 270 new nuclear reactors in the year 2030. This package of clean energy would reduce three times as much pollution as nuclear through 2030, for far less total cost.

Periodical and Internet Sources Bibliography

The following articles have been selected to supplement the diverse views presented in this chapter.

Thomas J. Billitteri	"Auto Industry's Future," *CQ Researcher*, February 6, 2009.
Ronald R. Cooke	"What Is the Real Cost of Corn Ethanol?" *Cultural Economist*, February 2, 2007.
Charles Duhigg	"Cleansing the Air at the Expense of Waterways," *New York Times*, October 12, 2009.
Jon Entine	"Coal and Climate Change: Can King Coal Clean Up?" *Ethical Corporation*, March 3, 2009.
Kenneth P. Green	"The Ethanol Delusion," *Pittsburgh Post-Gazette*, August 10, 2008.
Kurt Kleiner	"Nuclear Energy: Assessing the Emissions," *Nature Reports Climate Change*, September 24, 2008.
Alice McKeown	*The Dirty Truth About Coal*, Sierra Club, June 2007. www.sierraclub.org
New York Times	"A Reasonable Bet on Nuclear Power," February 17, 2010.
Lawrence Solomon	"The Dirty Truth," *National Post* (Canada), February 21, 2009.
Michael Totty	"The Case For and Against Nuclear Power," *Wall Street Journal*, June 30, 2008.

OPPOSING
VIEWPOINTS®
SERIES

CHAPTER 3

How Can Communities Reduce Pollution?

Chapter Preface

Government mandates that require the use of pollution-reducing goods and services are one controversial way in which communities can reduce pollution. Even if green goods and services cost more, some argue that because they reduce pollution, conserve energy, or keep waste out of landfills, governments should increase the demand for their use. Indeed, as of January 2008, twenty-six states adopted standards that required electricity generating companies to use a certain fraction of power from renewable fuels such as wind, solar, and biomass. Some would like to see a national mandate for these renewable portfolio standards (RPS). The House of Representatives in 2007 did pass an energy bill that included a 15 percent RPS requirement by 2020. The RPS provision was removed when critics claimed that it would increase electricity prices and penalize those regions with fewer renewable resources. Similar arguments are made concerning other green products and services. Indeed, one of the controversies in the debate over how communities can best reduce pollution is whether government interference helps or hinders community pollution-reduction efforts.

Supporters argue that government involvement can help reduce pollution by establishing content or performance standards and requirements. For example, they assert, building codes and energy efficiency standards for appliances help consumers make intelligent buying decisions. According to economics professor Thomas Tietenberg in a February 2008 article in *CQ Researcher*, "if you're walking around a house looking at it, you have no idea what kind of insulation is in the walls or how efficient the heating system is, but building codes set some basic thresholds for performance." Volunteer labeling programs, proponents claim, are a way to supplement codes and standards. For example, the Energy Star program, which is administered by the Environmental Protection Agency (EPA) and the Department of Energy, has set energy efficiency standards for consumer electronics, heating and cooling systems, and lighting. According to the EPA, in 2006 over 2 billion Energy Star products were sold, saving enough electricity to power more than 15 million American households for a year.

Opponents of government interference claim that reducing pollution is better left to the market. Manufacturers are in the best position to know how to create green products, these commentators claim. Indeed, they assert, state and federal government interference can lead to products that do not perform well. For example, when in 2007, the government required top-loading washers to meet energy efficiency standards, these washers initially received poor ratings in *Consumer Reports*. In a May 16, 2007, news release, the Competitive Enterprise Institute (CEI) claimed that the Department of Energy had ruined a perfectly dependable appliance. Even some environmentalists dispute the impact of green products. According to environmental author Bill McKibben in a 2007 article in *Mother Jones*, "If your appliances have gotten more efficient, there are also far more of them: The furnace is better than it used to be, but the average size of the house it heats had doubled since 1950. The 60-inch TV? The always-on cable modem? No need for you to do the math—the electric company does it for you, every month."

For many, the growth of green consumption demonstrates that environmental values are no longer a minority concern. However, the shift to promoting green, "checkbook" consumption in the eyes of many environmentalists runs counter to the belief that rampant economic growth and high consumption are the root environmental threat to the planet. The authors in the following chapter debate the effectiveness of other strategies communities might use to reduce pollution. "As a nation," says radio host and self-proclaimed "Lazy Environmentalist" Josh Dorfman, "we have neither the political leadership nor the political will, which is why I think that for now the environmental solutions presented have to be both effective and painless." How painless these solutions will be remains to be seen.

| "If our goal is to reduce carbon emissions as efficiently as possible, offsets make perfect economic sense."

Consumer-Purchased Carbon Offsets Will Reduce Carbon Emissions

Robert H. Frank

In the following viewpoint, Robert H. Frank asserts that purchasing carbon offsets is not only good for the environment but also makes economic sense. When consumers buy carbon offsets, they pay others who conduct non-carbon-emitting activities such as planting trees to offset the emissions consumers make driving and flying, for example. These economic incentives give people a reason to consider the environmental consequences of their actions, Frank maintains. Nevertheless, Frank reasons, certification programs are necessary to verify that offset purchasers actually offset carbon emissions. Frank, a Cornell University economist, is author of The Economic Naturalist's Field Guide: Common Sense Principles for Troubled Times.

Robert H. Frank, "Carbon Offsets: A Small Price to Pay for Efficiency," *New York Times*, May 31, 2009. Reproduced by permission.

As you read, consider the following questions:

1. In Frank's view, what might prevent some people from buying a hybrid car?

2. According to the author, what approach was first used in the United States to address acid rain?

3. How does the author contrast the impact of those who might use the hypothetical CheatNeutral to those who might buy carbon offsets?

A re carbon offsets a good thing?

They are intended to reduce the environmental impact of consumption. Traveling by plane, for example, causes carbon dioxide to be emitted into the atmosphere, so travelers can pay a specialist to offset those emissions some other way—perhaps by planting vegetation or installing renewable energy technologies. It all sounds reasonable.

Yet carbon offsets have drawn sharp criticism, even ridicule. A British website called CheatNeutral parodies the concept—by offering a service under which someone who wants to cheat on his partner can pay someone else who will refrain from committing an act of infidelity. The site's founders say they wanted to use humor to demonstrate why the market for carbon offset is a moral travesty.

Misguided Criticism

But the criticism is misguided. If our goal is to reduce carbon emissions as efficiently as possible, offsets make perfect economic sense.

Consider the decision of whether to buy a hybrid car. Because of the expensive batteries and other complex equipment in such cars, they can cost much more than similar vehicles powered by standard combustion engines. Many people drive so little that they wouldn't save enough on gasoline to recoup the higher cost. Yet many such people buy hybrids anyway, because they think they are helping the environment. Well and good, but they could help even more by buying a standard car and using the savings to buy carbon offsets.

The same goes for someone who wonders whether it's O.K. to eat foods grown far from home. A New Yorker may worry, for example, that the diesel fuel burned to ship California-grown tomatoes to him in winter will accelerate global warming. But suppose he would be happy to pay $10 more than the cost of shipping those tomatoes rather than eat locally grown root vegetables nine months a year. That would buy more than enough carbon offsets to neutralize the greenhouse gases emitted by shipping the tomatoes. So it would be much better, for him and the planet, if he bought offsets and ate winter tomatoes.

Of course, carbon offsets alone won't eliminate global warming. People also need stronger incentives to take into account the environmental consequences of their actions.

President [Barack] Obama has proposed attacking the problem with a carbon cap-and-trade system. The government would first set a limit on annual carbon emissions, then auction emissions permits to the highest bidders. Companies could still use processes or sell products that emit carbon, but only by first buying a permit for each unit of carbon released. If the government wanted to limit carbon emissions to five billion tons a year, for example, it would auction that many tons of annual carbon permits.

This approach was first used in the United States to address acid rain, when the Clean Air Act established a market for permits to emit sulfur dioxide. Compared with more traditional regulatory measures, the auction method substantially reduced the cost of achieving the law's air-quality target.

As people learn more about such an approach, they seem less likely to oppose it. Although several environmental groups once bitterly opposed pollution permit auctions, they now endorse them enthusiastically.

Reinforcing Other Carbon-Reduction Schemes

A carbon cap-and-trade system is functionally similar to a carbon tax. Both approaches would raise the cost of activities that generate carbon dioxide emissions, giving people a powerful incentive to reduce their carbon footprints. Carbon offsets are no substitute for the stronger incentives inherent in carbon taxes or cap and trade, but they can reinforce their effects. Both carbon taxes and permit auctions would also generate revenue that could be used to buy additional carbon offsets.

Dozens of companies, nonprofit and for-profit, sell carbon offsets, and some critics question how their work can be verified. But with various certification programs now in place—including the Gold Standard and Green-e Climate, to name two—there is no reason that fraud should be harder to curb in carbon-offset markets than in other domains.

At last count, CheatNeutral, the British infidelity neutralization website, said it had offset 65,768 cheats, and had recruited a roster of "9,002 faithful people ready to neutralize your misdemeanors." The website draws out the parallel this way: "When you cheat on your partner you add to the heartbreak, pain, and jealousy in the atmosphere." CheatNeutral claims that its plan "neutralizes the pain and unhappy emotion and leaves you with a clear conscience."

Actually, no. Only you will know whether your conscience is clear, but it is certain that higher rates of marital fidelity in London do nothing to eliminate the anguish caused by straying spouses in Manchester. In contrast, one person's reduction in carbon dioxide emissions anywhere on the planet fully offsets anyone else's contribution to the total.

Carbon offsets, though much maligned, are an excellent idea. If you want to help reduce carbon emissions, consider buying some.

> *"Individuals and businesses who are feeding a $700 million global market in [carbon] offsets are often buying vague promises instead of the reductions in greenhouse gases they expect."*

Consumer-Purchased Carbon Offsets Do Not Always Reduce Carbon Emissions

Doug Struck

Some carbon-offset programs fail to neutralize carbon dioxide emissions, maintains Doug Struck in the following viewpoint. Thus, some consumers who believe that they are neutralizing the carbon dioxide pollution that they emit when driving or flying may not in fact be doing so, he claims. The desire to help reduce the impact of carbon dioxide emissions has created a multi-million dollar industry with no rules or oversight, Struck argues. Unfortunately, he concludes, unscrupulous organizations have taken advantage of this opportunity, neutralizing few if any carbon emissions. Struck, who covered climate change for the Washington Post, is now a freelance writer and associate chair of journalism at Emerson College in Boston.

Doug Struck, "Buying Carbon Offsets May Ease Eco-Guilt but Not Global Warming," *Christian Science Monitor*, April 20, 2010. Reproduced by permission.

As you read, consider the following questions:

1. According to Struck, how was the Vatican fooled into thinking that its carbon emissions had been offset?

2. What did the US Government Accountability Office and a parliamentary inquiry in Britain reveal about carbon offsets, according to the author?

3. In the author's view, what is the result of a traveler paying for something that was going to be done anyway?

Tiszakeszi, Hungary—A forest was supposed to be here, inhaling carbon dioxide. But the fields are as empty as the promises of the carbon offsets that promoters said would help negate global warming with thousands of new trees near this Hungarian village.

An investigation by the *Christian Science Monitor* and the New England Center for Investigative Reporting [NECIR] has found that individuals and businesses who are feeding a $700 million global market in offsets are often buying vague promises instead of the reductions in greenhouse gases they expect.

They are buying into projects that are never completed, or paying for ones that would have been done anyhow, the investigation found. Their purchases are feeding middlemen and promoters seeking profits from green schemes that range from selling protection for existing trees to the promise of planting new ones that never thrive. In some cases, the offsets have consequences that their purchasers never foresaw, such as erecting windmills that force poor people off their farms.

Carbon offsets are the environmental equivalent of financial derivatives: complex, unregulated, unchecked and—in many cases—not worth their price.

Getting Fooled

And often, those who get the "green credits" thinking their own carbon emissions have been offset, are fooled. The Vatican was among them.

Cardinal Paul Poupard stood for the flash of cameras in the Vatican in the summer of 2007, beneath an image of Jesus healing a blind man, and accepted a gold-framed certificate declaring the papal city the "first carbon-neutral sovereign state."

By negating all the Vatican's 2007 greenhouse gas emissions with carbon offsets presented to the Holy See by the company KlimaFa, "the Vatican will do its small part in contributing to the elimination of polluting emissions . . . threatening the survival of this planet," the cardinal proclaimed.

No one was happier about it than Kiss Lajos. The stubby 65-year-old has presided as mayor of the scratch-poor farming village of Tiszakeszi in the Hungarian plains since the days of the Soviets.

For his constituents, who scavenge brush along the Tisza River for their home fires, the ceremony in the Vatican offered rare hope: The Hungarian company KlimaFa promised to hire hundreds of workers to plant thousands of trees near their village to suck up carbon on behalf of the Vatican.

It did not happen.

KlimaFa has not planted a tree on what it ambitiously dubbed "the Vatican Forest" in the Tiszakeszi countryside, even as the California promoter who started the company used the publicity to sell offsets on the Internet.

The Hungarian government, initially a cheerleader of the project, now does not want to talk about it. The company's president in Budapest backed out of an interview. The greenhouse gases produced by the cars and furnaces and lights of the papal apartments in the Vatican were not neutralized by the offsets. And a Vatican spokesman says "the case is being studied to take legal action in order to defend the Vatican's reputation."

"They were duped," says Jutta Kill, an analyst for FERN (Forests and European Union Resource Network), which tracks environmental scams. And the Vatican was hardly alone.

A Worldwide Market with No Rules

Tens of thousands of buyers purchase carbon offsets yearly to help neutralize their global warming pollution. They pay $5, $10, $20 or more from green-swathed sites on the Internet, or pay extra for offsets when they purchase airline tickets, rent a car, or ship a package. Companies buy them in bulk to help project a "green" image. Government agencies and civic organizations get offsets believing the purchases will make their actions "carbon neutral."

They have created a worldwide market estimated by analyst Ecosystem Marketplace at $705 million in 2008. In the United States alone, offset sales have tripled in five years.

But these offsets—some sold through respected environmental organizations—come with almost no rules: There is little regulatory oversight of them in the US, no enforcement of requirements to prove their environmental claims, no certain way of measuring the carbon savings being sold, and no guarantees that planted trees or other projects will be finished or continued long enough to work.

The result, critics say, is a "Wild West" market ripe for fraud, exaggeration, and poorly run projects.

The investigation by NECIR and the *Monitor* found examples of irregularities in the market that include:

- An offset project in India that cleared plots of traditional tribal farmlands to build windmills for green electric power, upending some farmers' livelihoods and—in the end—generating significantly less power than expected.

- A tree-planting project in Panama that promises profits for logging as well as calling itself a certified offset program when it is not. Few trees have even been planted.

- Scams in Australia that have prompted the alarmed government to launch a crackdown.

- A California promoter who launched a ship to spread iron dust in the South Pacific to grow carbon-sucking algae, a plan that the Environmental Protection Agency said would amount to illegal dumping at sea.

- An Israeli charity that is selling offsets that are supposed to create brand new projects, for tree plantings it has been doing for 60 years.

Such examples are causing some supporters of carbon offsets to back off what they once saw as a promising tool to help the environment. And the troublesome record concerns those who want a national carbon cap-and-trade program in the US that would use offsets.

"I think you are looking at 75 percent of them as garbage, at least," says Rolf Skar, a forest conservationist and senior investigator for Greenpeace in San Francisco.

Rapid Growth Ripe for Abuse

Some consumers are becoming wary. The US House of Representatives dropped plans to make its Capitol offices "carbon neutral" last year after spending $89,000 on offsets. Nike shoes abandoned them this year as untrustworthy. Responsibletravel .com, a British travel agency that claimed to be the first to offer carbon offsets in 2002 as a centerpiece of its business, has quit relying on them to help the environment. Instead, the company urges its clients to fly less.

The US Government Accountability Office (GAO) in 2008 found "limited assurance of credibility" in voluntary offsets. A parliamentary inquiry in Britain in 2007 found a long list of flaws with offsets and concluded that they have "no overarching, enforceable standards."

Australia takes the most vigorous stand: Regulators pounced on one company for selling offsets for renewable energy it did not have, they charged another with false practices;

Anything Goes

There is no government oversight of [carbon offset] sites, nor is there a uniform standard for what constitutes a legitimate offset. Price and quality vary greatly.

Some websites provide scant information about the criteria they use to pick projects and how much they charge for overhead, making it difficult for consumers to sort out effective offsets from projects that have little true environmental value.

"It really is anything goes," says Anja Kollmuss, outreach coordinator for the Tufts University Climate Initiative.

Beth Daley, "Carbon Confusion," Boston Globe, March 12, 2007.

and they are investigating allegations that natives in neighboring Papua New Guinea were deceived into surrendering carbon rights for what the natives call "sky money."

"This is a sector that's starting to rear a couple of ugly heads," says Graeme Samuel, head of the Australia's consumer protection agency.

Many voluntary carbon offsets are sold online through retailers with eco-friendly names. Others are sold as add-ons: Travel companies allow customers to "fly green," UPS customers can offset the cost of shipping packages, Ford car buyers can drive "carbon neutral" for $29.95 per year, and the Harvard Law School urges students to buy offsets when they travel for job interviews.

A Reluctance to Abandon Offsets

Greenpeace and other environmental organizations have been reluctant to completely reject carbon offsets, which are supposed to help achieve goals they support: drawing down greenhouse gas levels in the atmosphere, protecting forests, promoting alternative energy, and encouraging individual action on the global climate problem.

Groups such as the Nature Conservancy, the Environmental Defense Fund, and the Sierra Club argue that some offset projects are run by well-intentioned developers and succeed in their claims. And offset retailers say they do good work.

"There is a great opportunity here to be able to subsidize the reduction of emissions," says Pete Davies, president of the retail operations of TerraPass, a San Francisco offset provider that helps farmers pay for methane capture systems. "We see farmers being able to do the right thing that otherwise they wouldn't be able to do. We're excited to be a part of that."

The appeal of doing something to help the environment has fed the rapid growth of offset sales.

"I buy them every time I fly," says Matt Durden, a Reston, Va., attorney who figures he spends about $30 on carbon offsets through Expedia when he and his wife travel. He did not ponder the purchases long; they seemed a cheap and easy way to help the environment, he says.

Governments worldwide are contemplating mandatory offset programs, like that established in Europe under the Kyoto agreement. A top United Nations climate official predicted in 2006 that buying and selling carbon pollution reductions would become a $100 billion-a-year market, potentially the world's largest commodities market.

Voluntary purchases are a small part of that, but even a small slice of such a big pie has created a burgeoning industry of offset developers, wholesalers, retailers, and promoters; the GAO counted at least 600 players in the US alone in 2008.

Mr. Skar, of Greenpeace, says the industry is rife with financial speculators in flannel shirts: "Carbon cowboys. People from the most bizarre backgrounds. People who have no prior interest in the environment."

How It Works

The theory of carbon offsets is straightforward. For example, a traveler who generates a ton of carbon dioxide pollution by driving about 2,000 miles in an average car can purchase an offset to pay for the reduction of a ton of carbon dioxide somewhere else in the world. The offset might promise that trees will be planted, methane digesters will be installed on farms, or new windmills will be financed by the purchase.

Where the reduction occurs doesn't matter, proponents argue, as long as the atmosphere is relieved of that ton of carbon. Others are queasy about the notion of paying to relieve their environmental responsibility.

Carol King Cummings, a Poison, Mont., retiree thinks of the offset concept this way: "My great-great-grandfather paid someone to fight for him in the Union Army in the US Civil War. This always embarrassed me a little. Carbon offsets strike me the same way."

For the theory to work, several requirements must be met. The most vexing is that the traveler's purchase must create a reduction in greenhouse gas emissions that would not have happened without the traveler's money. If the traveler pays for something that was going to be done anyway, that is double-counting and the traveler's emissions are not offset.

This requirement of "additionality" has been difficult to apply, and critics say many projects are selling offsets to reap bonus profits for projects already being created for other purposes.

Windmill farms, for example, typically are built only if they can sell the electricity and also get substantial government subsidies or tax credits. On expensive projects like these, offset developers typically provide a small portion of the construction cost. Critics say the projects would probably go ahead with other funding, so developers should not claim credit for creating new carbon reductions.

"It might sound great, like a wind farm. Who can be against a wind farm?" says Anja Kollmuss, who has studied offsets for the nonprofit Stockholm Environment Institute. "But wind farms are very likely to have been built for something else. For the consumer, it's incredibly difficult to understand."

The Jewish National Fund (JNF), for example, has been urging Jews worldwide to "plant a tree in Israel" since 1948. Now, it is offering a "GoNeutral" calculator to figure how many trees one needs to offset one's carbon emissions. JNF says one $10 tree over a lifetime of 70 years will absorb one ton of emissions.

"What the JNF is doing carbon-wise is not additional. Anything you do that is business-as-usual is not eligible for a carbon-offset purchase," protests Eyal Biger, the founder of the Good Energy Initiative, a nonprofit Israeli organization that also sells offsets for trees. Mr. Biger's group contends its trees are planted in urban areas, and are therefore new and additional.

Rabbi Eric Lankin, a JNF official, contends the GoNeutral purchases pay to plant trees beyond the group's business-as-usual quota. But he acknowledges the rules on trees and offsets are hazy: "The challenge is that this is not an exact science."

Not an Exact Science

Others reject the theoretical underpinning of offsets: They are created by claiming to do something that would not normally have been done, and then predicting how much carbon would be produced with—and without—that action.

"The trouble is nobody can really verify—unless you can read a crystal ball—what would have happened. There are an infinite number of possibilities," says Ms. Kill, at FERN.

Offsets also are required to be permanent, or reasonably close to it. Carbon dioxide, the largest component of greenhouse gases, may last for 100 years in the atmosphere. But off-setting a ton of carbon dioxide by planting trees, vulnerable to destruction, does not assure permanence.

"Trees get blown down by wind. They burn in forest fires. They are eaten up by insects. The trees are harvested, or they die from old age," says Kill. "Forests are probably the worst pick" for offsets. They are, however, a favorite of promoters because of their symbolic appeal. According to Ecosystem Marketplace, forestry projects in 2008 spawned an estimated 5 million tons of offsets at an average price of $8.44 per ton.

But if forests are cut or destroyed, there is no legal re-quirement—and little incentive—for the buyer or the seller to replace the lost carbon savings, Kill notes.

"You take a holiday and you want to offset your flight. You go to one of these terminals or online, and you buy your car-bon credits. What's the potential of you as an individual—unless you are extremely dedicated or skilled—to find out what exactly is happening to the project in five or 10 years' time?" Kill asks.

Paying Not to Cut Trees

Critics also question where the money provided by offset pur-chases really goes. With no regulatory oversight, there is no disclosure of profit margins, and the finances of offset provid-ers are shrouded in claims of confidentiality. The analytic firm Ecosystem Marketplace says the industry "resembles the Wall Street of the 1800s—with information closely guarded by those who profit from it."

The San Francisco offset provider 3Degrees, for example, sells offsets through an ATM-like kiosk recently installed, with much publicity, at the San Francisco International Airport. Travelers can use the machine to offset emissions from their flights—at $13.50 a carbon ton—expecting to buy a new car-bon savings somewhere.

In fact, they are paying 3Degrees to send money to two environmental groups—the Nature Conservancy and the Conservation Fund—for a promise not to cut down trees on land the environmental groups already own. The groups estimate how much carbon would be lost if they opened their northern California forest to logging, and they sell that amount as an "offset."

Jason Brown, a spokesman for 3Degrees, declined to say how the offset sales are split.

Silva Tree, a promoter that sells plots of trees in Panama, takes the opposite tack. It promises investors that it will plant trees in Panama that will be logged in five years, bringing "guaranteed" returns of $145,200 if they pay $32,500 now for a hectare (2.5 acres) with 660 trees. Investors cannot buy offsets. But Silva Tree advertising and telephone sales personnel say that the project involves, or will involve, certified carbon offsets. Sales representatives suggest that hundreds of acres of the "biggest reforestation project in Panama" have been planted. In a visit to the site with Silva Tree contractors in February, the *Monitor* found only about 25 acres planted.

Such uncertainties worry officials like Javier Arias, the environmental minister of Panama. The government must be vigilant so that what companies "say is going to happen, must happen," he said in an interview. "Everybody pays for a bad apple."

Even offset providers acknowledge the industry is rife with abuses. "There's a lot of bad stuff going around," says Roger Ryall, who sells offsets to car dealerships in Canada. "There are guys out there planting grass and trying to sell offsets from it. You have to be careful."

"If it is carried out correctly, electronics recycling can prevent pollution, create jobs, and save resources."

Recycling Innovation Will Reduce E-Waste Pollution

Valerie Thomas

In the following viewpoint, Valerie Thomas asserts that recycling policies that support innovation during the complete electronics supply chain can reduce electronic waste pollution. Engineering innovation in the manufacturing process can reduce pollution before electronic products even enter the market, she maintains. A standardized label that identifies the product and its components will make recycling easier for consumers and recyclers, Thomas argues. Rather than spend money educating consumers on device-specific recycling requirements, electronic products with smart labels could manage the recycling process themselves, she reasons. Thomas, a professor in the School of Industrial and Systems Engineering at Georgia Institute of Technology, studies product life cycle management.

Valerie Thomas, "Electronic Waste: Investing in Research and Innovation to Reuse, Reduce and Recycle," Testimony Before the Committee on Science and Technology, US House of Representatives, February 11, 2009. Reprinted by permission.

As you read, consider the following questions:

1. In Thomas's opinion, why is the use of information technology to manage the end-of-life supply chain of electronic products especially important?

2. According to the author, what are some of the benefits to manufacturers and retailers of radio-frequency identification codes?

3. In the author's view, what remains to be done with respect to engineering education?

Disposal or recycling of electronics can have significant human health and environmental impacts. Electronics can contain lead, brominated flame retardants, cadmium, mercury, arsenic and a wide range of other metals and chemical compounds. The recycling rate is, at best, about 18%, and most electronics collected in the U.S. for recycling have been sent to other countries for processing. In a 2008 report, the GAO [Government Accountability Office] found that a substantial fraction of these end up in countries where disposal practices are unsafe to workers and dangerous to the environment. Used electronics exported from the United States to some Asian countries are dismantled under unsafe conditions, using methods like open-air incineration and acid baths to extract metals such as copper and gold.

If it is carried out correctly, electronics recycling can prevent pollution, create jobs, and save resources. Keeping activities such as sorting and reprocessing of electronics in the urban areas where they have been used and collected can provide significant economic and social benefits. These benefits could be significantly enhanced if plans for recycling and refurbishment were incorporated into the design of the product and its supply chain.

Not Currently Designed for Recycling

It is widely recognized that electronics have not been designed for recycling: The valuable components are hard to extract and difficult to reuse, and the valuable constituents are mixed with a complex set of low value and potentially hazardous materials.

What is less well recognized is that the electronics supply chain also has not been designed for recycling. The existing supply chain for manufacturing, delivery, and retailing of electronics is a model of efficiency, managed with electronic data interchange, electronic manifests, radio-frequency tags on pallets and cartons, and UPC [Universal Product Code] codes on individual product packages. These kinds of supply chain innovations, developed over the past thirty years, have saved money and allowed for the efficient production and retailing of tens of thousands of products. In stark contrast, the end-of-life supply chain is managed almost entirely by hand, with little record keeping or even potential for monitoring or oversight. That the result has included unsafe, polluting, and illegal disposal activities should not be a surprise.

Electronics are just one example of the myriad products that consumers and businesses are increasingly expected to recycle. Recent major efforts to encourage electronics recycling have brought the recycling rate up to about 18%. Major efforts to encourage recycling of batteries—including passage of the 1996 Mercury-Containing and Rechargeable Battery Management Act—have been even less successful. The draft E-Waste R&D Act [Electronic Waste Research and Development Act] proposes to address low recycling rates by "studying factors that influence behavior and educating consumers about electronic waste." This will not be nearly enough. To achieve high collection rates, recycling programs for consumer products such as electronics and batteries will need a different approach to collection.

A Need for Supply Chain Innovation

If electronics—or any other complex or hazardous products—are going to be recycled as part of a planned and well-managed system, supply chain renovation is needed. Use of information technology to manage the end-of-life supply chain will be especially important because there are thousands of different makes and models of electronics products that enter the waste stream every year.

Electronics—and other complex products that need to be recycled—could have a standardized label that would allow recyclers to identify the make and model of the product and manage its recycling or refurbishment. These labels could be something like a standard UPC bar code. Alternatively, a radio-frequency identification code (RFID) could be installed inside the product and serve the same function while being easier to read and providing more information.

In a small project sponsored by the US EPA [Environmental Protection Agency] and convened by the RFID standards organization, EPCglobal, recyclers, electronics manufacturers, and retailers are beginning to think through how electronics recycling could be improved by use of RFID tags. This is an ongoing project, but in our preliminary report, the group has concluded that potential benefits for manufacturers and retailers include:

- increased efficiency and lower cost for recycling,
- opportunities for recycling incentives, rebates, coupons and trade-ins,
- improved warranty management, and
- better after-sale services.

Potential benefits for recyclers include:

- improved inventory control,

- more efficient product sorting and management,

- improved audit capabilities,

- integration of product data into online markets, and

- easier and less costly reporting to regulators and clients.

Better management of today's recycling programs is only the beginning of what could be accomplished. The end-of-life management of electronics and other products could be transformed by a combination of improved product design, innovative online markets, integration of information technology into product management, and supply chain innovations. Already, online markets such as eBay, Craigslist, and Freecycle have made the reuse and refurbishment of electronics easier and more common. Already, companies like RecycleBank use RFID codes on recycling bins to reward consumers for recycling.

In the future, consumers could start the process of recycling, reuse or resale simply by putting their unwanted item in their own "smart" recycling bin: The bin would automatically read the label on the product, and automatically arrange for recycling pickup; the recycler, receiving information in advance about the items in the bin, would be able to automatically arrange for sorting and resale or recycling, and the consumer would receive a rebate for recycling that specific item, based on its value or hazard. This kind of system places the capability to enter the collection system within the product itself. Rather than having to continue to work so hard to educate consumers about how to recycle each and every one of their purchases, consumer products could, almost, manage themselves.

Creating Products That Manage Their Own Recycling

Today, recycling programs for electronics and other consumer products have low recycling rates both because collection pro-

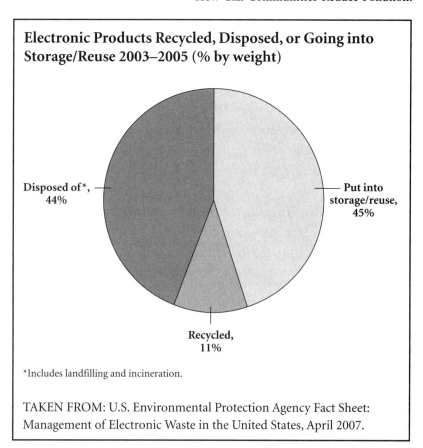

Electronic Products Recycled, Disposed, or Going into Storage/Reuse 2003–2005 (% by weight)

Disposed of*, 44%

Put into storage/reuse, 45%

Recycled, 11%

*Includes landfilling and incineration.

TAKEN FROM: U.S. Environmental Protection Agency Fact Sheet: Management of Electronic Waste in the United States, April 2007.

grams are difficult for consumers to use and because the products are difficult to recycle. To achieve high recycling rates, products need to be designed for recycling, and collection programs need to be designed to be very easy, almost automatic, regardless of the complexity of the product. Currently, *consumers* are mainly responsible for managing the recycling or disposal of their products. In some locations there have been efforts to make *producers* responsible for managing the recycling or disposal of their products. A third approach might work better: improve both product design and collection systems so that *products* can increasingly manage their own entry into the collection and recycling system.

With respect to the specifics of the legislation: The draft E-Waste R&D Act will be most effective if it takes into account the entire life cycle of electronics products. Electronics can have environmental impacts in manufacturing and in use as well as in disposal. Use of recycled materials or components can reduce the environmental impact of electronics production. In some cases reusing or refurbishing electronics will result in more energy use than would purchase of a new model; in other cases used or refurbished electronic devices can provide more environmental, economic and social benefit than recycling. A research program that focuses only on end of life has the potential to overlook major opportunities for reducing the environmental impacts of electronics, and could be counterproductive. The research program should consider the full life cycle of electronics.

With respect to engineering education: The engineering 2020 study from the National Academy of Engineering has identified environmental issues as one of the key challenges facing the world and the engineering profession now and in the coming decades. Equally importantly, students realize that this is important, and courses related to energy, environment, and sustainability can draw students in to the field of engineering. Section 6 of the draft E-Waste R&D Act supports the consideration of environmental consequences in undergraduate and graduate-level engineering curriculum. Many institutions of higher education have already made substantial progress in this area. A recent survey shows that teaching and research in sustainable engineering are part of the activities of most of the top 100 engineering programs in the United States. At my own institution, the Georgia Institute of Technology, almost every school in the College of Engineering has environmental offerings at both the undergraduate and graduate level. Yet there is much to be done. By and large, the environmental aspects of the engineering curricula are at an introductory level. The next step is to develop the depth and rigor that engineers will need, and that engineering departments will require for environmental material to be adopted into their core curricula. Engineering schools are well prepared to take the next steps, and support for this work would be welcomed.

"Green infrastructure has a number of environmental and economic benefits in addition to reducing sewer overflows and stormwater discharges."

Green Urban Stormwater Infrastructure Can Reduce Waterway Pollution

Nancy Stoner

Traditional development practices have led to urban stormwater runoff that pollutes American waterways, claims Nancy Stoner in the following viewpoint. Green infrastructure, on the other hand, mimics the natural water cycle, she asserts. Instead, Stoner urges the development of soil and vegetation that can be worked into the urban landscape in the form of rain gardens, porous pavements, and vegetated median strips. These technologies keep rainwater out of the sewer system and thus prevent sewer overflow, she argues. Green infrastructure also reduces flooding, air pollution, and urban temperatures, she contends. Stoner is codirector of the water program at the Natural Resources Defense Council, an environmental advocacy group.

Nancy Stoner, "Efforts to Address Urban Stormwater Runoff," Testimony Before the Subcommittee on Water Resources and Environment, March 19, 2009. Courtesy of the Subcommittee on Water and Resources and Environment Concerns.

As you read, consider the following questions:

1. In Stoner's opinion, how is climate change stressing aquatic ecosystems, infrastructure, and water supplies in much of the United States?

2. How does green infrastructure enhance water supplies, according to the author?

3. In the author's view, how does green infrastructure protect surface water quality?

Interest in green infrastructure is skyrocketing among members of Congress, the sewage treatment industry, state and local governments, and the public. This is an opportune moment to discuss the barriers to full, effective implementation of green infrastructure as an integral part of water and wastewater resources management in communities across the country.

The Problem of Urban Stormwater Runoff

Many communities, ranging from highly developed cities to newly developing towns, are looking for ways to assure that their rivers, streams, lakes, and estuaries are protected from the impacts of urbanization and climate change. Traditional development practices cover large areas of the ground with impervious surfaces such as roads, driveways, and rooftops. Once such development occurs, rainwater cannot infiltrate into the ground, but rather runs off-site at levels that are much higher than would naturally occur. The collective force of all such rainwater scours streams, erodes stream banks, and causes large quantities of sediment and other pollutants to enter the water body each time it rains.

In addition to the problems caused by stormwater and non-point source runoff, many older cities (including many of the largest cities in the United States), have combined sewage and stormwater pipes which periodically and in some cases frequently overflow due to precipitation events. In the late 20th century, most cities that attempted to reduce sewer overflows did so by separating combined sewers, expanding treatment capacity or storage within the sewer system, or by replacing broken or decaying pipes. However, these traditional practices can be enormously expensive and take decades to implement. Moreover, piped stormwater and combined sewer overflows ("CSOs") may also in some cases have the adverse effects of upsetting the hydrological balance by moving water out of the watershed, thus bypassing local streams and groundwater. Many of these events also have adverse impacts and costs on source water for municipal drinking water utilities.

Climate change is already stressing aquatic ecosystems, infrastructure, and water supplies. While impacts vary regionally, in much of the U.S., more frequent heavy rainfall events overload the capacity of sewer systems and water and wastewater treatment plants, as well as result in more stormwater runoff, exacerbating water pollution from sediments, nutrients, pathogens, pesticides, and other pollutants. In addition, decreased summer precipitation and other changes to the volume and timing of flows reduce stored water in reservoirs and reduce groundwater levels. Sea-level rise will adversely affect groundwater by causing an increase in the intrusion of salt water into coastal aquifers. All of these impacts will make less fresh water available for human use.

A Need for New Techniques

To ameliorate these problems, a set of techniques, approaches and practices can be used to eliminate or reduce the amount of water and pollutants that run off a site and ultimately are discharged into adjacent water bodies. We refer to these collectively as "green infrastructure." As cities move towards sustainable infrastructure, green infrastructure can be a valuable approach.

"Green infrastructure" is a relatively new and flexible term, and it has been used differently in different contexts. Thus, to date, there is no universally established definition of the term. For example, some writers have defined it broadly as "an interconnected system of natural areas and other open spaces that conserve natural ecosystem values and functions, sustains clean air and water, and provides a wide array of benefits to people and wildlife." The Green Infrastructure Statement of Intent signed by U.S. EPA [Environmental Protection Agency], NRDC [Natural Resources Defense Council], the Low Impact Development Center, the National Association of Clean Water Agencies (NACWA) and the Association of State and Interstate Water Pollution Control Administrators (ASIWPCA) uses the term "green infrastructure" to generally refer to systems and practices that use or mimic natural processes to infiltrate, evapotranspirate (the return of water to the atmosphere either through evaporation or by plants), or reuse stormwater or runoff on the site where it is generated.

What Is Green Infrastructure?

Green infrastructure involves management approaches and technologies that utilize, enhance and/or mimic the natural hydrologic cycle processes of infiltration, evapotranspiration and reuse. Green infrastructure is the use of soil, trees, vegetation, and wetlands and open space (either preserved or created) in urban areas to capture rain while enhancing wastewater and stormwater treatment. Green infrastructure approaches currently in use include green roofs, trees and tree boxes, rain gardens, vegetated swales, pocket wetlands, infiltration planters, porous and permeable pavements, vegetated median strips, reforestation/revegetation, and protection and enhancement of riparian buffers and floodplains. Green infrastructure can be used almost anywhere soil and vegetation can be harnessed or worked into the urban or suburban landscape. Green infrastructure also includes decentralized

rainwater harvesting approaches, such as the use of rain barrels and cisterns to capture and reuse rainfall for watering
plants or flushing toilets. These approaches can be used to
keep rainwater out of the sewer system so that it does not
contribute to a sewer overflow and also to reduce the amount
of untreated runoff discharging to surface waters. Green infrastructure also allows stormwater to be absorbed and cleansed
by soil and vegetation and either reused or allowed to flow
back into groundwater or surface water resources.

Green Infrastructure Benefits

Green infrastructure has a number of environmental and economic benefits in addition to reducing sewer overflows and
stormwater discharges, including:

Cleaner Water—Percolation of stormwater through soil,
uptake by vegetation, and water reuse reduce the volumes of
stormwater runoff and, in combined systems, the volume of
combined sewer overflows, as well as reduce concentrations of
pollutants in those discharges.

Enhanced Water Supplies—Most green infiltration approaches involve allowing stormwater to percolate through the
soil where it recharges the groundwater and the base flow for
streams, thus ensuring adequate water supplies for humans
and more stable aquatic ecosystems. In addition, capturing
and using stormwater conserves water supplies.

Reduced Flooding—Green infrastructure both controls surface flooding and stabilizes the hydrology so that peak stream
flows are reduced.

Cleaner Air—Trees and vegetation improve air quality by
filtering many airborne pollutants and can help reduce the
amount of respiratory illness. Green infrastructure approaches
that facilitate shorter commute distances and the ability to
walk to destinations also reduce vehicle emissions.

Reduced Urban Temperatures—Summer city temperatures
can average 10°F higher than nearby suburban temperatures.

High temperatures are also linked to higher ground-level ozone concentrations. Vegetation creates shade, reduces the amount of heat-absorbing materials and emits water vapor—all of which cool hot air. Limiting impervious surfaces, using light colored impervious surfaces (e.g., porous concrete), and vegetating roofs also mitigate urban temperatures.

Moderated Impacts of Climate Change—Climate change impacts and effects vary regionally, but green infrastructure techniques provide adaptation benefits for a wide array of circumstances, by conserving and reusing water, promoting groundwater recharge, reducing surface water discharges that could contribute to flooding. In addition, there are mitigation benefits such as reduced energy demands and carbon sequestration by vegetation.

Increased Energy Efficiency—Green space helps lower ambient temperatures and, when incorporated on and around buildings, helps shade and insulate buildings from wide temperature swings, decreasing the energy needed for heating and cooling. Also energy use associated with pumping and treating is reduced as stormwater is diverted from wastewater collection, conveyance and treatment systems. Energy efficiency not only reduces costs, but also reduces generation of greenhouse gases.

Source Water Protection—Green infrastructure practices provide pollutant removal benefits, thereby providing some protection for both groundwater and surface water sources of drinking water. In addition, green infrastructure provides groundwater recharge benefits by putting stormwater back into the ground and enhances surface water quality by redirecting the high volume and velocity flows that scour streams and muddy drinking water sources.

Wildlife Habitat—Stream buffers, wetlands, parks, meadows, green roofs, and rain gardens increase biodiversity within the urban environment.

Community Benefits—Trees and plants improve urban aesthetics and community livability by providing recreational and wildlife areas. Studies show that property values are higher, homes sells faster, and crime is reduced when trees and other vegetation are present.

Health Benefits—Studies show that people who have access to green infrastructure in their communities get more exercise, live longer, and report better health in general. Exposure to green infrastructure (even through a window) improves mental functioning, reduces stress, and reduces recovery time from surgery.

Green Jobs—Designing, installing, and maintaining green infrastructure creates new jobs for architects, designers, engineers, construction workers, maintenance workers, plumbers, landscapers, nurseries, etc.

Cost Savings—Green infrastructure saves capital costs associated with paving, curb and gutter, building large collection and conveyance systems, and digging big tunnels and centralized stormwater ponds; operations and maintenance expenses for treatment plants, pumping stations, pipes, and other hard infrastructure; energy costs for pumping water around; cost of treatment during wet weather; and costs of repairing the damage caused by stormwater, such as streambank restoration. . . .

Communities across the U.S. are poised to use green infrastructure to revive their waterways, revitalize their neighborhoods, and create green jobs, but there are significant barriers that they face in adopting green infrastructure solutions. Thank you for holding this hearing today to explore those barriers and Congress's role in removing them. I appreciate the opportunity to appear before you to address these issues and look forward to your questions.

Periodical and Internet Sources Bibliography

The following articles have been selected to supplement the diverse views presented in this chapter.

Jeffrey Ball	"Six Products, Six Carbon Footprints," *Wall Street Journal*, October 6, 2008.
Thomas J. Billitteri	"Mass Transit Boom," *CQ Researcher*, January 18, 2008.
Thomas J. Billitteri	"Reducing Your Carbon Footprint: Can Individual Actions Reduce Global Warming?" *CQ Researcher*, December 5, 2008.
Ben Elgin	"Little Green Lies," *BusinessWeek*, October 29, 2007.
Todd Litman	"Comprehensive Analysis of Transit Energy Conservation Benefits," Planetizen.com, May 27, 2008. www.planetizen.com.
Mark Lynas	"Can Shopping Save the Planet?" *Guardian* (UK), September 17, 2007.
Rachel Nowak	"'Total Recycling' Aims to Make Landfill History," *New Scientist*, October 20, 2007.
Michael Specter	"Big Foot," *New Yorker*, February 25, 2008.
Jennifer Weeks	"Future of Recycling," *CQ Researcher*, December 14, 2007.
Alex Williams	"Don't Let the Green Grass Fool You," *New York Times*, February 10, 2008.

OPPOSING VIEWPOINTS® SERIES

CHAPTER 4

What Federal Policies Will Best Reduce Pollution?

Chapter Preface

One of the oldest debates over what federal policies will best reduce pollution is whether environmental regulations hinder or help improve air quality. In fact, since Congress passed the Clear Air Act in 1970, environmental activists and energy industries have disputed its impact and effectiveness. When the auto industry was required to install catalytic converters on all new vehicles to reduce tailpipe emissions, industry representatives predicted that the regulation would bankrupt automakers. Despite these fears, the regulation resulted in new technological advances that reduced converter costs and emissions. In fact, in its 2003 report to Congress on the costs and benefits of federal regulatory decisions, the Office of Management and Budget reported that the Clean Air Act led to $146 to $230 billion in benefits at a cost of only $36 to $42 billion. Regardless, when in 2002 then President George W. Bush proposed his "Clear Skies" initiative, commentators on both sides of the controversial proposal renewed the debate over the effectiveness of federal involvement in pollution control.

Bush's proposal relaxed the rule that required older power plants be refitted with modern pollution-control technology when the companies that owned these plants decided to modernize. In addition, the proposed Clear Skies Act allowed power companies to choose between installing emission-reducing equipment and buying pollution credits from cleaner plants. When Congress did not pass the Clear Skies Act, the Bush administration asked the Environmental Protection Agency (EPA) to create rules that that would help implement many of his proposals. Several states, local governments, and environmental groups challenged these EPA rules, and lower federal courts vacated these rules in 2008; the Supreme Court has yet to rule on their constitutional validity.

Those who support these less restrictive pollution reduction policies argue that federal technology requirements actually increase pollution. They believe that these requirements discourage energy providers from increasing production or developing their own environmentally friendly technologies. Under the strict rules of the Clean Air Act, if power companies choose to modernize, they must add expensive new power-generating equipment, these analysts assert. Thus, they reason, in many cases, rather than install expensive equipment, energy companies continue to operate these polluting power plants without modernizing. Those who oppose federal regulation also argue that as energy demands have grown, air pollution has decreased and thus increasingly strict federal restrictions are an unnecessary burden on power companies. According to Dan Riedinger, spokesperson for the Edison Electric Institute, the primary lobbying organization of the utility industry, "No matter how well-intended, no regulation the EPA issues can provide the same certainty for businesses or the environment."

Those who support federal regulation to reduce pollution argue that efforts to subvert the Clean Air Act will reverse air quality improvements. Outdated power plants "give our kids asthma, taint our fish with mercury and cause the premature death of thousands of Americans a year," claims Connecticut senator Joe Lieberman in a September 15, 2003, press release. Lieberman states that relaxed rules have the effect of praising plants that pollute rather than insisting that they reduce dangerous pollutants. When in November 2003, the EPA dropped numerous investigations into Clear Air Act air pollution violations, environmental groups and states that are particularly pollution ridden filed suit. In a public statement on November 6, 2003, then New York attorney general Eliot Spitzer argued, "my office formed a partnership with the federal government to reduce air pollution from power plants. . . . That effort is now at risk." The fight to reestablish the strict pollution-reduction policies of the original Clean Air Act begun during the Bush administration continues in the US courts.

Those on both sides of the debate over whether federal regulations help or hinder pollution efforts await the Supreme Court's decision on the latest clear air policies. The authors in the following chapter debate the effectiveness of other federal strategies designed to reduce dangerous pollutants while America's energy needs grow.

> *"Going forward, the oil industry must be required to meet a high standard for safety and training, and government agencies need to ensure that they meet those standards."*

Increased Federal Oversight of Offshore Oil Drilling Is Necessary to Prevent Pollution

Times-Picayune (New Orleans, LA)

Federal oversight of the offshore oil industry is necessary to protect US waters from pollution, argue the editors of the Times-Picayune, a New Orleans, Louisiana, newspaper, in the following viewpoint. Current policies allow the oil industry to police itself, the authors maintain. This lack of oversight contributed to the 2010 explosion of the Deepwater Horizon offshore oil rig that is polluting the waters of the Gulf of Mexico, the authors claim. Policy makers must also require high standards of safety and training and make sure that these standards are met, the authors reason.

Times-Picayune [New Orleans, LA], "Federal Oversight of Oil Industry Is Broken," May 16, 2010. © 2010 The Times-Picayune Publishing Co. All rights reserved. Used with permission of *The Times-Picayune*.

As you read, consider the following questions:

1. In the editors' opinion, what happened when the Minerals Management Service inspector visited the Deepwater Horizon before the April 20, 2010, explosion?

2. According to the authors, to what is the Minerals Management lapse painfully reminiscent for South Louisianians?

3. What approach, used in the United Kingdom and Norway, do the authors claim makes sense?

As investigators began last week [May 2010] looking into the explosion and sinking of the Deepwater Horizon [an oil rig located off the Louisiana coast], the testimony became a litany of what wasn't done.

Officials from the Minerals Management Service [MMS] said their agency didn't require BP[1] or any other companies to verify that so-called blowout preventers would actually work.

An oil industry group sets standards for the safety devices, but MMS doesn't do anything to ensure that the standards are met. When there is a concern about blowout preventers, the agency usually issues written notices that are not enforceable.

The MMS inspector who most recently visited the Deepwater Horizon was a trainee who said he didn't make note of any equipment readings taken that day. The agency also does little to determine whether crew members on a rig are capable of doing their jobs. There are no licensing requirements for crucial jobs—and when MMS inspectors conduct on-site tests of rig workers to see if they are qualified, there is no follow-up to ensure that a worker who fails gets more training.

1. BP is a British global energy company that the U.S. government has held responsible for the explosion of the Deepwater Horizon, a drilling rig owned and operated by Transocean Ltd. on behalf of BP.

Collective Frustration

Tougher oversight rules were written nine years ago [in 2001] but never adopted, so the oil industry essentially is left to police itself.

With every revelation, Coast Guard Capt. Hung Nguyen—one of six hearing officers—sounded more exasperated.

"So, MMS approves the design of the well, but they don't check what type of pipe is used," Capt. Nguyen said. "And we have a study some time ago about whether a shear ram would cut a certain pipe (to shut off a well in an emergency), but we don't know what was installed here. I don't understand that."

Capt. Nguyen could have been expressing the collective frustration of South Louisiana. Offshore drilling is an inherently dangerous endeavor, but the Minerals Management Service did little or nothing to ensure a standard of safety that might have protected coastal Louisiana and the rest of the Gulf Coast from a disastrous spill.

For South Louisianians, the Minerals Management lapses are painfully reminiscent of the shoddy work by the U.S. Army Corps of Engineers that led to the deadly collapse of federal floodwalls during [Hurricane] Katrina [in 2005]. Lt. Gen. Carl Strock admitted the corps's missteps before he retired from the agency in 2006. "This has been sobering for us, because for the first time the corps has had to stand up and say we had a catastrophic failure with one of our projects."

Vowing to Increase Federal Oversight

President Obama on Friday [May 14, 2010] acknowledged that Minerals Management is also culpable in the Gulf oil spill and he announced a review of MMS's actions. The president vowed to end the "cozy relationship" between companies and the agency, saying MMS issued drilling permits "based on little more than assurances of safety from the oil companies. That cannot and will not happen anymore."

The president must make sure of that.

Interior Secretary Ken Salazar already has announced plans to split MMS, which is under his control, into two pieces: one entity to monitor safety of offshore operations and the other to handle oil leases and the collection of royalty payments. That approach, which is used in the United Kingdom and Norway, makes sense. Having one agency in charge of safety and new exploration puts it at cross-purposes.

But Secretary Salazar needs to do more than slice Minerals Management down the middle. The agency was known to be a mess before its ineptitude and impotence were detailed at the hearing in Kenner last week.

During his tenure at the Gulf regional office in Louisiana for the MMS, Chris Oynes played a central role in an offshore leasing foul-up that cost taxpayers an estimated $10 billion in lost revenue. The Interior Department's inspector general called the matter "a jaw-dropping example of bureaucratic bungling." Despite that, the agency's then director promoted Mr. Oynes in 2007 to associate director for the offshore program.

In a separate inquiry in 2008, the inspector general described the Minerals Management Service as having a "culture of ethical failure" that led to lax collection of royalties and improper relationships with the industry. When he became interior secretary last year, Mr. Salazar ended a controversial royalty-in-kind program that was the target of Inspector General Earl Devaney's 2008 findings. Mr. Devaney outlined an inappropriate relationship between some MMS employees in Washington and Colorado and representatives of the oil industry, including sexual encounters.

The testimony this week in Kenner didn't reveal anything of that order. But the agency's New Orleans District drilling engineer testified that he was unaware of an MMS regulation that requires drilling companies to submit proof that a well's blowout preventer will have enough power to shear a drill pipe in case of an emergency. He said he has never demanded that sort of proof in any of the more than 100 applications his office reviews annually.

The so-called shear arms on the blowout preventer at the Deepwater Horizon have failed repeatedly to cut the pipe and close off the leak.

Blowout preventers are not the first line of defense in an underwater accident, but MMS and the industry should make sure that the equipment is capable of shutting off a well.

Going Forward

At a U.S. Senate hearing Tuesday [May 11, 2010], executives from BP, Transocean and Halliburton[2] all said it was too early to determine a precise cause for the Deepwater Horizon explosion, but each of them also pointed fingers at each other. That isn't helpful.

What is most important at this point, of course, is to stem the oil pouring into the Gulf. Investigations into the cause, or

2. Halliburton was in charge of cementing during the construction of the Deepwater Horizon.

causes, of the accident will take time to sort through what promises to be voluminous amounts of evidence.

It is already clear, though, that federal oversight was virtually nonexistent, and safety suffered because of it. Going forward, the oil industry must be required to meet a high standard for safety and training, and government agencies need to ensure that they meet those standards.

Twice in the past five years, South Louisianians have ended up in dire straits because institutions that were supposed to protect us didn't. That should never happen again.

| "The accelerating speed of [oil technology] innovation seems to be outstripping government regulators' capacity to deal with risks, much less anticipate them."

Offshore Oil Drilling Technologies Are Too Challenging to Regulate

Kenneth Rogoff

In the following viewpoint, Kenneth Rogoff claims that offshore oil technologies can be so complex that attempts to regulate them can actually limit innovation. Trying to balance the need for energy and environmental protection can lead to regulations that are either too strict or not strict enough, he asserts. Indeed, Rogoff reasons, overreaction to the 2010 Deepwater Horizon offshore oil disaster may impede technological development in the energy industry. The challenge is even greater in developing nations, where economic growth often takes a priority over environmental concerns, he concludes. Rogoff, professor of economics and public policy at Harvard University, was formerly chief economist at the International Monetary Fund.

Kenneth Rogoff, "Oil Spill's Lessons for Regulation," *Business World*, 2010. Reproduced by permission.

As you read, consider the following questions:

1. In Rogoff's opinion, what parallels can be drawn between the oil spill and the recent financial crisis? How are these crises similar?

2. According to the author, what is the impact of the BP oil spill on the promise of extending oil supplies for another generation?

3. In the author's view, what problems must be better understood to avoid being doomed to regulation that over- or undershoots its goals?

As the damaged BP oil well continues to spew millions of gallons of crude from the depths of the floor of the Gulf of Mexico, the immediate challenge is how to mitigate an ever-magnifying environmental catastrophe. One can only hope that the spill will be contained soon, and that the ever-darkening worst-case scenarios will not materialize.

The disaster, however, poses a much deeper challenge to how modern societies deal with regulating complex technologies. The accelerating speed of innovation seems to be outstripping government regulators' capacity to deal with risks, much less anticipate them.

The parallels between the oil spill and the recent financial crisis are all too painful: the promise of innovation, unfathomable complexity, and lack of transparency (scientists estimate that we know only a very small fraction of what goes on at the oceans' depths). Wealthy and politically powerful lobbies put enormous pressure on even the most robust governance structures. It is a huge embarrassment for US President Barack Obama that he proposed—admittedly under pressure from the Republican opposition—to expand offshore oil drilling greatly just before the BP catastrophe struck.

A Seductive Story

The oil technology story, like the one for exotic financial instruments, was very compelling and seductive. Oil executives bragged that they could drill a couple of kilometers down, then a kilometer across, and hit their target within a few meters. Suddenly, instead of a world of "peak oil" with ever-depleting resources, technology offered the promise of extending supplies for another generation.

Western officials were also swayed by concerns about the stability of supplies in the Middle East, which accounts for a large proportion of the world's proven reserves. Some developing countries, most notably Brazil, have discovered huge potential offshore riches.

Now all bets are off. In the United States, offshore drilling seems set to go the way of nuclear power, with new projects being shelved for decades. And, as is often the case, a crisis in one country may go global, with many other countries radically scaling back offshore and out-of-bounds projects. Will Brazil really risk its spectacular coastline for oil, now that everyone has been reminded of what can happen? What about Nigeria, where other risks are amplified by civil strife?

Oil experts argue that offshore drilling never had the potential to amount to more than a small share of global supply. But there now will be greater concerns about deep drilling in *any* sensitive environment. And the problem is not just with oil. The big news in energy these days is the revolution in technology for tapping shale gas. With important reserves near populated areas, governments will need to temper their enthusiasm and think about the balance between risks and riches.

The basic problem of complexity, technology, and regulation extends to many other areas of modern life. Nanotechnology and innovation in developing artificial organisms offer a huge potential boon to mankind, promising development of new materials, medicines, and treatment techniques. Yet, with all of these exciting technologies, it is extremely difficult to strike a balance between managing "tail risk"—a very small risk of a very large disaster—and supporting innovation.

Financial crises are almost comforting by comparison. Speculative bubbles and banking crises have been a regular feature of the economic landscape for centuries. Awful as they are, societies survive them.

True, people who thought, "This time is different," before the recent Great Recession were proven wrong. But, even if we are not getting any better at dealing with financial crises, things have not necessarily been getting worse, either.

Perhaps the G-20 [Group of Twenty, finance ministers from twenty wealthy nations] government leaders have not done quite as brilliant a job plugging the hole in the financial system as they claim. The raging sovereign-debt problems in continental Europe, and the brewing ones in the US, Japan, and elsewhere are proof enough of that. But, compared to British Petroleum's [BP's] efforts to plug its deep-sea oil hole, the G-20 leaders look omnipotent.

If ever there were a wake-up call for Western society to re-think its dependence on ever-accelerating technological innovation for ever-expanding fuel consumption, surely the BP oil spill should be it. Even China, with its "boom now, deal with the environment later" strategy should be taking a hard look at the Gulf of Mexico.

Economics teaches us that when there is huge uncertainty about catastrophic risks, it is dangerous to rely too much on the price mechanism to get incentives right. Unfortunately, economists know much less about how to adapt regulation over time to complex systems with constantly evolving risks, much less how to design regulatory resilient institutions. Until these problems are better understood, we may be doomed to a world of regulation that perpetually overshoots or under-shoots its goals.

The finance industry already is warning that new regulation may overshoot—that is, have the unintended effect of sharply impeding growth. Now, we may soon face the same concerns over energy policy, and not just for oil.

Given the huge financial stakes involved, achieving global consensus will be difficult, as the Copenhagen climate-change fiasco[1] proved. The advanced countries, which can best afford to restrain long-term growth, must lead by example. The balance of technology, complexity, and regulation is without doubt one of the greatest challenges that the world must face in the twenty-first century. We can ill afford to keep getting it wrong.

---

1. The 2009 United Nations meeting on climate change at Copenhagen, in the eyes of many, failed to lead to any significant progress on global climate change policy. Some analysts believe the Copenhagen accord lacks teeth.

> *"Allowing the market to set a price on pollution will shift investments toward clean technologies and improved efficiency, while unleashing Americans' unique talent for . . . technological ingenuity."*

Federally Mandated Cap-and-Trade Policies Will Reduce Air Pollution

John Podesta

Cap-and-trade policies will create the corporate incentives needed to reduce pollution, maintains John Podesta in the following viewpoint. Caps, he asserts, limit the pollutants that corporations can put into the air, and trade policies allow those companies that reduce their pollution to trade their permits to others. Allowing the market to set a price on pollution will promote investment in technologies that create less pollution, Podesta claims. Investment in clean technologies will in turn promote economic growth, he concludes. Podesta is president and chief executive officer of the Center for American Progress, a progressive public policy research and advocacy organization.

John Podesta, "Cap-and-Trade Will Reduce Global Warming and Create Jobs," *U.S. News & World Report*, August 18, 2009. Reproduced by permission.

As you read, consider the following questions:

1. According to Podesta, how did the United States pioneer the cap-and-trade concept?

2. How much does the author claim the ACES Act will cost the average household when efficiency measures are factored in?

3. In the author's opinion, what will be the net increase in jobs as the result of the ACES Act combined with the American Recovery and Reinvestment Act?

On June 26 [2009], the House of Representatives passed comprehensive energy legislation that included, for the first time in U.S. history, a cap on global warming pollution. The bill, called the American Clean Energy and Security [ACES] Act, would also boost investments in energy efficiency and renewable energy, like wind and solar, to jump-start the transition to a clean energy economy. New investments in the clean energy technologies of the future would slash global warming pollution and reduce the use of foreign oil while also creating jobs and increasing our economic competitiveness vis-à-vis China and other nations.

The so-called ACES Act would implement a cap-and-trade system to reduce global warming pollution and spur investment in clean energy technologies. Today, corporations can freely dump global warming pollution into the atmosphere while society foots the bill for the ill effects. The act would limit the amount of global warming pollution that corporations could freely release into the air. Congress would set steadily declining emissions limits, and polluters would have to obtain permits for every ton of pollution they produced—in essence, a "dumping permit" for the sky. Corporations that reduce global warming pollution below their allotment could then sell an equivalent value of permits back to the open market. This system thus empowers individuals, entrepreneurs, and businesses to determine where necessary emissions reductions are most efficiently found.

A Product of American Ingenuity

The cap-and-trade concept itself is a product of American ingenuity. The United States pioneered it in the 1990 Clean Air Act to force power plants to reduce sulfur dioxide pollution, which causes acid rain. The program, developed during the first Bush administration, was a complete success—meaning it achieved total compliance in reducing sulfur dioxide pollution—and cost as little as one-fifth of the Environmental Protection Agency's original $6 billion forecast. Both the gross domestic product and total electricity generation continued to rise at a steady clip after the program began. And despite claims that the limits on sulfur dioxide pollution would cause electricity bills to rise, rates are lower now (in constant dollars) than in 1990. Finally, the success of our first cap-and-trade program means that, today, we don't have to worry about—or pay for—the negative health effects, damaged infrastructure, and poor crop yields that acid rain would have caused if we'd chosen to do nothing.

We stand at a similar crossroads today, but we've cleaned our environment while driving economic growth many times before. The Congressional Budget Office estimates that the House legislation will cost the average household only $175 annually—the equivalent of a postage stamp a day. It will cost even less when efficiency measures are factored in, which would save families about 7 percent—or $84—annually on their electric bills. The act also includes provisions to protect low-income families and farmers from any potential cost increases.

A Catalyst for Innovation

But the bill is designed to do much more than reduce global warming pollution at an affordable cost. It will also catalyze clean energy innovation on a remarkable scale. Allowing the

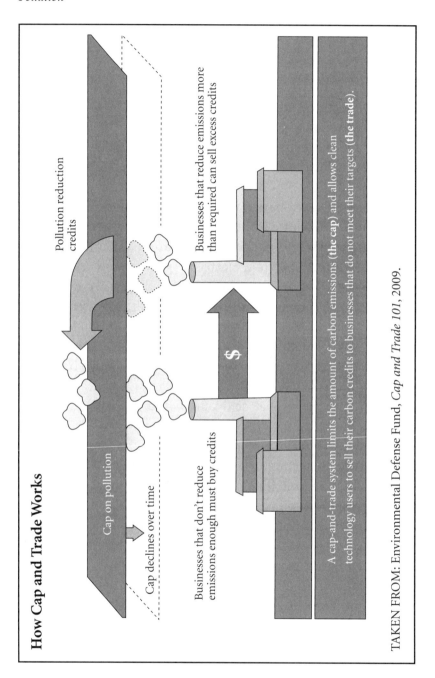

How Cap and Trade Works

Pollution reduction credits

Cap on pollution

Cap declines over time

Businesses that don't reduce emissions enough must buy credits

Businesses that reduce emissions more than required can sell excess credits

$

A cap-and-trade system limits the amount of carbon emissions (**the cap**) and allows clean technology users to sell their carbon credits to businesses that do not meet their targets (**the trade**).

TAKEN FROM: Environmental Defense Fund, *Cap and Trade 101*, 2009.

market to set a price on pollution will shift investments toward clean technologies and improved efficiency, while unleashing Americans' unique talent for problem solving and technological ingenuity. The United States will join Europe and China—already bounding ahead—to capitalize on the most significant economic opportunity since the United States dominated the information technology revolution in the 1990s.

To make sure the United States can lead the world during the coming era of clean energy, the act creates a Clean Energy Deployment Administration—simply put, a "Green Bank." This program would provide clean energy projects with steady, low-cost credit to accelerate the development and commercialization of new technologies. It would use well-understood financial tools to work hand in hand with the private sector to boost lending and investment in a diverse range of clean energy projects that would otherwise have difficulty accessing steady, affordable commercial financing. And it would allow the United States to catch up to countries like China, which is already investing more than 3 percent of its total GDP [gross domestic product] in green programs, compared with America's current investment of less than one half of 1 percent.

Creating New Jobs

The innovation, development, and commercialization of new clean energy technologies will bring millions of new jobs for people at all skill levels to communities across the country. The act, combined with the American Recovery and Reinvestment Act, would yield a net increase of 1.7 million new jobs in manufacturing, construction, and other sectors. And we know that one dollar invested in clean energy creates four times as many jobs as that same dollar invested in the energy industries of the past. Clean energy jobs have already shown impressive growth, even during difficult economic times; they experienced annual increases of nearly 10 percent from 1998 to 2007, more than 2 ½ times the rate of overall job growth.

Stories around the country already are bearing these statistics out. Retrofitting initiatives, supported by the recovery act, are putting local communities to work making homes and office buildings more energy efficient; wind turbine manufacturers in Michigan are hiring former auto employees to build complex power-generation machinery.

The House of Representatives has already done its part to make sure millions of Americans will have similar stories to tell. Now, it's the Senate's turn to support comprehensive energy legislation that will cap and reduce global warming pollution, create jobs, and put America's economy on a smart, clean, and competitive path forward.

> "*[Cap-and-trade laws] will cause economic harm without producing any environmental or climate-protective benefits.*"

Federally Mandated Cap-and-Trade Policies Will Not Reduce Air Pollution

Kenneth Green

In the following viewpoint, Kenneth Green asserts that the reasoning behind cap-and-trade policies is unsound. For example, he reasons, since energy demand grows as the economy grows, policies that reduce energy production, such as caps on carbon emissions, in turn reduce, rather than promote, growth. Moreover, cap-and-trade policies encourage cheating, Green asserts. In fact, he maintains, firms in the United States and Europe have overstated past emissions and exaggerated the benefits of new technologies to obtain permits to trade. Green is a fellow at American Enterprise Institute for Public Policy Research, a libertarian think tank.

Kenneth P. Green, "How Not to Address Climate Change," *TCS Daily*, January 30, 2008. Reproduced by permission.

As you read, consider the following questions:

1. In Green's opinion, on what basis are supporters of cap-and-trade calling for domestic cap-and-trade legislation? Why is this reasoning faulty?

2. What does economist Margo Thorning claim will be necessary to meet the emission reduction targets of the Warner-Lieberman Climate Security Act?

3. In the author's opinion, why will governments not want to look very hard to validate a company's claimed historic emissions?

Common sense should tell us that good policies produce more in benefits than they cost us. Unfortunately, common sense has left the building when it comes to climate policy. Asserting (somewhat absurdly) that America's economic and geopolitical competitors, such as China and India, are just waiting for "U.S. moral leadership," several voices are renewing their call for domestic cap-and-trade legislation to control greenhouse gases.

But cap-and-trade schemes are fundamentally flawed, and particularly ill suited to greenhouse gas control. The current poster child for cap and trade is the Warner-Lieberman Climate Security Act of 2007 (S. 2191). If enacted, Warner-Lieberman will cause economic harm without producing any environmental or climate-protective benefits. This is the hallmark of irrational policy.

Unrealistic Goals

First, let's look at the likelihood that the legislation's goals can be met. Economist Margo Thorning observed in congressional testimony, "In order to meet the emission reduction targets in S. 2191, U.S. per capita emissions would have to fall by a total of 13.8 percent over the 2000–2012 period, an additional 20.2 percent from 2012 to 2020 and a further 27.6 from 2020 to

2030. In other words, the required reductions in per capita emissions are about 25 to 35 times greater than what occurred from 1990 to 2000. The technologies simply do not exist to reduce total (and per capita emissions) over the next 17 years by the amounts mandated in S. 2191. . . ." Thorning is not alone in this belief: in a 2004 *Science* article, a team of 18 prestigious scientists observed that meeting projected growth in energy demand while sharply curbing greenhouse gas emissions requires carbon-free technologies that "do not exist operationally or as pilot plants."

Now, let's look at the costs. Economist Anne Smith testified to Congress that her state-of-the-art economic modeling estimates that Warner-Lieberman would cause net reduction in 2015 GDP [gross domestic product] of 1.0% to 1.6% relative to the GDP that would otherwise occur. That loss rises to the range of 2% to 2.5% after 2015. Smith found that the annual loss in GDP would increase to the range of $800 billion to $1 trillion, which is serious money. By 2020, Smith estimates losses of 1.5 to 3.4 million jobs—and that is net jobs, after adjusting for the new "green" jobs that might be created by the bill.

None of this is surprising as experience has shown cap-and-trade schemes are fundamentally flawed. Here are four reasons. First, capping carbon essentially puts a regulatory drag on economic growth. When the economy grows, energy demand rises, which means the demand for the limited number of carbon permits would rise, strangling growth in its cradle.

Encouraging Cheaters and Raising Costs

Second, everyone involved in a cap-and-trade system has incentives to cheat. Companies have incentives both to overstate historical emissions, and to exaggerate the benefits of new technologies to generate bogus emissions that become ready cash. Experience in both the US and Europe shows that firms

The Problem with Unilateral Efforts

As time goes on, the United States will emit a smaller and smaller share of the world's total greenhouse gas emissions, which makes unilateral efforts—such as a domestic cap-and-trade program—an ineffective way to influence climate. If the United States were to completely cease using fossil fuels, the increase from the rest of the world would replace U.S. emissions in less than eight years.

Institute for Energy Research,
"Cap and Trade Primer: Eight Reasons Why Cap
and Trade Harms the Economy and Reduces Jobs,"
March 12, 2009.

usually get away with it: Validating historic emissions is nearly impossible. And governments won't look very hard—wanting to appear green, they have strong incentives to turn their eyes away from carbon credit malfeasance.

Third, cap-and-trade creates a perpetual group of rent seekers—those raking in profits in new carbon trading—who will call for ever-tighter caps, and who will staunchly oppose any other approach to dealing with greenhouse gas emissions. Once a company holds millions of dollars in carbon credits, they can be expected to spend large sums of money lobbying against anything that would devalue their new currency.

Finally, carbon cap and trade will raise the costs of energy, goods, and services. If that does not happen, there is no incentive for anyone to cut back on energy use, and the attendant emissions it produces. This could be offset, in theory, if the carbon permits were all auctioned off, and the revenues used to lower other taxes. But no emission trading system has ever auctioned off a majority of permits, and Warner-

Lieberman is no exception: At first, it auctions only a trivial share of emission permits, and even when that ramps up decades hence, the revenues are used as a wealth-redistribution tool focused mainly on funding dubious energy research schemes rather than protecting the overall economy from the impact of higher energy prices.

The post-Bali refrain is that the US should "lead" by enacting carbon cap and trade. Apart from the silliness of assuming that our economic and political competitors are waiting on the US for "moral leadership," carbon cap and trade is simply bad policy: Its costs are high, and benefits nonexistent. Rational climate policy would consist of a short-term focus on adaptation, and a longer-term effort to reduce greenhouse gas emissions via a modest revenue-neutral carbon tax.

> *"Because coal liquefaction processes remove contaminants from coal prior to combustion, process emissions from coal-to-liquids plants are much lower than traditional pulverized coal power plants."*

The US Government Should Subsidize Liquid Fuel Production from Coal

John N. Ward

John N. Ward claims in the following viewpoint that since coal is abundant in the United States, investing in coal-to-liquids technology, also known as coal liquefaction, makes sense. Unlike other new energy technologies, coal liquefaction is well tested, he asserts. Because coal liquefaction processes remove pollutants from coal prior to combustion, the process is environmentally friendly, Ward maintains. Moreover, he argues, coal liquefaction lends itself well to carbon capture and storage, thus producing fewer greenhouse gas emissions than petroleum products. Ward is vice president of Headwaters Incorporated, a clean coal technology provider.

John N. Ward, "Improving America's Energy Security Through Liquid Fuels Derived from Coal," Testimony Before the Subcommittee on Energy and Environment, Committee on Science and Technology, US House of Representatives, September 5, 2007. Courtesy of the US Representatives Committee on Science & Technology.

As you read, consider the following questions:

1. According to Ward, why is coal-to-liquids fuel attracting so much attention today?

2. In what ways are coal-to-liquids refineries similar to petroleum refineries, in the author's view?

3. What does the author say would be the impact of utilizing coal and biomass together?

It's easy to see why coal-to-liquids is attracting so much attention these days. In the president's [George W. Bush's] words, the United States is addicted to oil. U.S. petroleum imports in 2005 exceeded $250 billion. In the past two years [2005–2007], natural disasters have disrupted oil production and refining on the U.S. Gulf Coast. Political instability in the Middle East and other oil-producing regions is a constant threat. Fuel prices have rapidly escalated along with world oil prices that are reaching levels unseen since the 1970s' energy crisis.

Why Coal-to-Liquids Fuel?

The situation is not likely to get much better in the future. Global oil demand was 84.3 million barrels per day in 2005. The United States consumed 20.7 million barrels per day (24.5%) and imported 13.5 million barrels per day of petroleum products. Worldwide demand for petroleum products is expected to increase 40% by 2025 largely due to growing demand in China and India. World oil production could peak before 2025. Most of the remaining conventional world oil reserves are located in politically unstable countries.

In contrast, coal remains the most abundant fossil fuel in the world and the United States has more coal reserves than any other country. With coal-to-liquids technology, the United States can take control of its energy destiny. Any product made from oil can be made from coal. At today's oil prices, coal-to-liquids is economical and has the power to enhance energy security, create jobs here at home, lessen the U.S. trade deficit, and provide environmentally superior fuels that work in today's vehicles. By building even a few coal-to-liquids plants, the U.S. would increase and diversify its domestic production and refining base—adding spare capacity to provide a shock absorber for price volatility.

A Historical Perspective

Headwaters [Incorporated, an energy services company] and its predecessors have been engaged in coal-to-liquids technologies since the late 1940s. Our alternative fuels division is comprised of the former research and development arm of Husky Oil and holds approximately two dozen patents and patents pending related to coal-to-liquids technologies.

The founders of this group included scientists engaged in the Manhattan Project during World War II. After the conclusion of the war, these scientists were dispatched to Europe to gather information on technologies used by Germany to make gasoline and diesel fuel from coal during the war.

In the late 1940s, this group designed the first high temperature Fischer-Tropsch conversion plant, which operated from 1950 to 1955 in Brownsville, Texas. It produced liquid fuels commercially at a rate of 7,000 barrels per day. Why did it shut down? The discovery of cheap oil in Saudi Arabia.

The Arab oil embargo of 1973 reignited interest in using domestic energy resources such as coal for producing transportation fuels. From 1975 to 2000, Headwaters researchers were prime developers of direct coal liquefaction technology. This effort, which received more than $3 billion of federal research funding, led to the completion of an 1,800 barrels per day demonstration plant in Catlettsburg, Kentucky. Why did deployment activities cease there? OPEC [Organization of the Petroleum Exporting Countries] drove oil prices to lows that left new technologies unable to enter the market and compete.

Today, our nation finds itself in another energy crisis. Oil costs more than $70 per barrel and comes predominantly from unstable parts of the world. There is little spare production and refining capacity and our refineries are concentrated in areas susceptible to natural disasters or terrorist attacks. And once again, our nation is considering coal as a source for liquid transportation fuels. The question is: What can we do this time to ensure that the technologies are fully deployed?

Reviewing the Coal-to-Liquids Technology

From a product perspective, coal-to-liquids refineries are very similar to petroleum refineries. They make the same range of products, including gasoline, diesel fuel, jet fuel and chemical feedstocks. These fuels can be distributed in today's pipelines without modification. They can be blended with petroleum-derived fuels if desired. They can be used directly in today's cars, trucks, trains and airplanes without modifications to the engines.

From a production perspective, coal-to-liquids refineries utilize technologies that have been commercially proven and are already being deployed in other parts of the world. Two main types of coal-to-liquids technologies exist. Indirect coal liquefaction first gasifies the solid coal and then converts the gas into liquid fuels. Direct coal liquefaction converts solid coal directly into a liquid "syncrude" that can then be further refined into fuel products. . . .

Direct coal liquefaction involves mixing dry, pulverized coal with recycled process oil and heating the mixture under pressure in the presence of a catalyst and hydrogen. Under these conditions, the coal transforms into a liquid. The large coal molecules (containing hundreds or thousands of atoms) are broken down into smaller molecules (containing dozens of atoms). Hydrogen attaches to the broken ends of the molecules, resulting in hydrogen content similar to that of petroleum. The process simultaneously removes sulfur, nitrogen and ash, resulting in a synthetic crude oil (syncrude) which can be refined just like petroleum-derived crude oil into a wide range of ultra-clean finished products. . . .

Indirect coal liquefaction is a two-step process consisting of coal gasification and Fischer-Tropsch (FT) synthesis. Coal is gasified with oxygen and steam to produce a synthesis gas (syngas) containing hydrogen and carbon monoxide. The raw syngas is cooled and cleaned of carbon dioxide and impurities. In the FT synthesis reactor, the cleaned syngas comes in contact with a catalyst that transforms the diatomic hydrogen and carbon monoxide molecules into long-chained hydrocarbons (containing dozens of atoms). The FT products can be refined just like petroleum-derived crude oil into a wide range of ultra-clean finished products. . . .

The Coal-to-Liquids Environmental Profile

Fuels produced by coal-to-liquids processes are usable in existing engines without modifications and can be distributed through existing pipelines and distribution systems. Nevertheless, they are exceptionally clean when compared to today's petroleum-derived transportation fuels.

Indirect coal liquefaction fuels derived from the Fischer-Tropsch process, in particular, contain substantially no sulfur and also exhibit lower particulate and carbon monoxide emissions. These fuels also contribute less to the formation of nitrogen oxides than petroleum-derived fuels and they are readily biodegradable.

The production of coal-to-liquids fuels is also environmentally responsible. Because coal liquefaction processes remove contaminants from coal prior to combustion, process emissions from coal-to-liquids plants are much lower than traditional pulverized coal power plants.

Both direct and indirect coal liquefaction plants generate carbon dioxide in highly concentrated form allowing carbon capture and storage. Coal-to-liquids plants with carbon diox-

Direct Coal Liquefaction

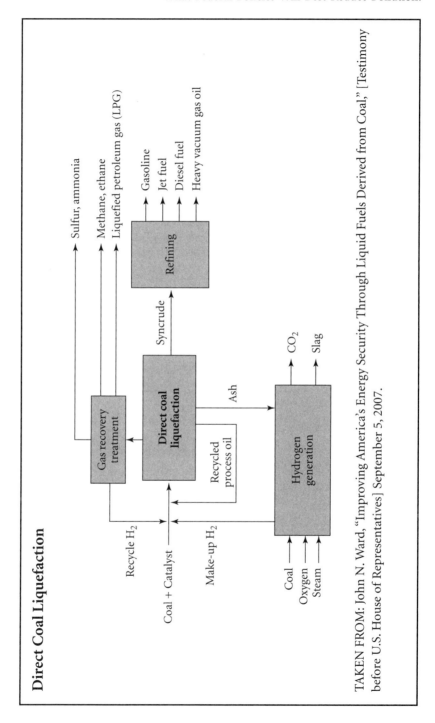

TAKEN FROM: John N. Ward, "Improving America's Energy Security Through Liquid Fuels Derived from Coal," [Testimony before U.S. House of Representatives] September 5, 2007.

ide capture and storage can produce fuels with life cycle greenhouse gas emission profiles that are as good as or better than that of petroleum-derived products.

Reducing Greenhouse Gas Emissions

A life cycle greenhouse gas emissions inventory for indirect coal liquefaction diesel was prepared for the U.S. Department of Energy National Energy [Technology] Laboratory (NETL) in June 2001. This study compared the emissions for indirect coal liquefaction (with and without carbon capture and storage) diesel with conventional petroleum diesel delivered to Chicago, IL. . . .

Life cycle greenhouse gas emission inventories have not been completed on direct and hybrid coal liquefaction technologies. However, based on the fact that these technologies have lower plant CO_2 [carbon dioxide] emissions than indirect coal liquefaction and the CO_2 is in concentrated form, it can be assumed that direct and hybrid technologies will have lower life cycle GHG [greenhouse gas] emissions than conventional petroleum diesel.

Gasification technologies like those that would be used in coal-to-liquids plants have already demonstrated the ability to capture and store carbon dioxide on a large scale. For example, the Dakota Gasification facility in North Dakota captures CO_2 from the gasification process and transports it by pipeline to western Canadian oil fields where it is productively used for enhanced oil recovery.

There is also growing interest in utilizing coal and biomass (agricultural and forestry by-products) together to further reduce net carbon dioxide emissions. This is achieved because biomass is considered a renewable resource and a zero net carbon dioxide emitter. The coprocessing of coal and biomass would allow a much greater scale of liquid fuel production than an exclusive reliance on biofuels.

The coprocessing of coal and biomass in commercial gasification plants is being done in Europe in the range of 80 to 90 percent coal and 10 to 20 percent biomass. It is speculated that up to 30 percent of the feed mix could be in the form of biomass; however there are economic and logistic issues to consider. Biomass is a bulky material with low density, high water content and is expensive to transport and pre-process for gasification. In addition, it tends to be seasonal and widely dispersed. . . .

The advantages to developing a coal-to-liquids capability in the United States are numerous. Some of the dollars we now send overseas to buy oil would be kept at home to develop American jobs utilizing American energy resources. We would expand and diversify our liquid fuels production and refining capacity using technologies that are already proven. We would produce clean-burning fuels that can be distributed through our existing pipelines and service stations to fuel our existing vehicles with no modifications to their engines. We would take a real and immediate step toward greater energy security.

> *"The U.S. can have a robust and effec-*
> *tive program to reduce oil dependence*
> *without rushing into an embrace of*
> *coal-to-liquids technologies."*

The US Government Should Not Subsidize Liquid Fuel Production from Coal

David G. Hawkins

In the following viewpoint, David G. Hawkins maintains that there is no evidence to prove that coal-to-liquids technology is clean or will reduce air pollution. Therefore, he argues, the government should not subsidize liquid fuels from coal. In fact, Hawkins claims, the total life cycle emissions of liquid coal technologies exceeds the greenhouse gas emissions of crude oil. Moreover, Hawkins asserts, no standards are in place to ensure that coal-to-liquids plants would control the emission of sulfur oxides, particulate matter, and other hazardous pollutants. Hawkins is director of the Climate Center at the Natural Resources Defense Council, an environmental advocacy organization.

David G. Hawkins, "Testimony of . . . Before Committee on Energy and Natural Resources," United States Senate, April 24, 2006. Courtesy of the US Senate Committee on Energy & Natural Resources.

As you read, consider the following questions:

1. In Hawkins's opinion, what types of assessments are needed before we decide if it is possible to use coal to make liquid fuels?

2. According to the author, what is the total "well-to-wheels" CO_2 emission rate from coal-to-liquids plants?

3. In the author's view, why are the particulate matter emissions in western surface mines particularly serious?

NRDC [Natural Resources Defense Council] fully agrees that reducing oil dependence should be a national priority and that new policies and programs are needed to avert the mounting problems associated with today's dependence and the much greater dependence that lies ahead if we do not act. A critical issue is the path we pursue in reducing oil dependence: a "green" path that helps us address the urgent problem of global warming and our need to reduce the impacts of energy use on the environment and human health; or a "brown" path that would increase global warming emissions as well as other health and environmental damage. In deciding what role coal might play as a source of transportation fuel NRDC believes we must first assess whether it is possible to use coal to make liquid fuels without exacerbating the problems of global warming, conventional air pollution and impacts of coal production and transportation.

If coal were to play a significant role in displacing oil, it is clear that the enterprise would be huge, so the health and environmental stakes are correspondingly huge. The coal company Peabody Energy is promoting a vision that would call for production of 2.6 million barrels per day of synthetic transportation fuel from coal by 2025, about 10% of forecasted oil demand in that year. According to Peabody, using coal to achieve that amount of crude oil displacement would require construction of 33 very large coal-to-liquids plants, each plant consuming 14.4 million tons of coal per year to produce 80,000 barrels per day of liquid fuel. Each of these plants would cost $6.4 billion to build. Total additional coal production required for this program would be 475 million tons of coal annually—requiring an expansion of coal mining of 43% above today's level. . . .

Global Warming Pollution

To avoid catastrophic global warming the U.S. and other nations will need to deploy energy resources that result in much lower releases of CO_2 [carbon dioxide] than today's use of oil, gas and coal. To keep global temperatures from rising to levels not seen since before the dawn of human civilization, the best expert opinion is that we need to get on a pathway now to allow us to cut global warming emissions by 60–80% from today's levels over the decades ahead. The technologies we choose to meet our energy needs in the transportation sector and in other areas must have the potential to perform at these improved emission levels.

To assess the global warming implications of a large coal-to-liquids program we need to examine the total life cycle or "well-to-wheel" emissions of these new fuels. Coal is a carbon-intensive fuel, containing double the amount of carbon per unit of energy compared to natural gas and about 50% more than petroleum. When coal is converted to liquid fuels, two streams of CO_2 are produced: one at the coal-to-liquids production plant and the second from the exhausts of the vehicles that burn the fuel. As I describe below, with the technology in hand today and on the horizon it is difficult to see how a large coal-to-liquids program can be compatible with the low-CO_2-emitting transportation system we need to design to prevent global warming.

Today, our system of refining crude oil to produce gasoline, diesel, jet fuel and other transportation fuels, results in a total "well-to-wheels" emission rate of about 27.5 pounds of

CO_2 per gallon of fuel. Based on available information about coal-to-liquids plants being proposed, the total well-to-wheels CO_2 emissions from such plants would be about 49.5 pounds of CO_2 per gallon, nearly twice as high as using crude oil, if the CO_2 from the coal-to-liquids plant is released to the atmosphere. Obviously, introducing a new fuel system with double the CO_2 emissions of today's crude oil system would conflict with the need to reduce global warming emissions. If the CO_2 from coal-to-liquids plants is captured, then well-to-wheels CO_2 emissions would be reduced but would still be higher than emissions from today's crude oil system.

This comparison indicates that using coal to produce a significant amount of liquids for transportation fuel would not be compatible with the need to develop a low-CO_2-emitting transportation sector unless technologies are developed to significantly reduce emissions from the overall process. But here one confronts the unavoidable fact that the liquid fuel from coal contains the same amount of carbon as is in gasoline or diesel made from crude. Thus, the potential for achieving significant CO_2 emission reductions compared to crude is inherently limited. This means that using a significant amount of coal to make liquid fuel for transportation needs would make the task of achieving any given level of global warming emission reduction much more difficult. Proceeding with coal-to-liquids plants now could leave those investments stranded or impose unnecessarily high abatement costs on the economy if the plants continue to operate.

Conventional Pollution

Conventional air emissions from coal-to-liquids plants include sulfur oxides, nitrogen oxides, particulate matter, mercury and other hazardous metals and organics. While it appears that technologies exist to achieve high levels of control for all or most of these pollutants, the operating experience of coal-to-liquids plants in South Africa demonstrates that coal-to-liquids

Technologically Achievable Oil Savings (million barrels per day)

Oil savings measures	2015	2025
Raise fuel efficiency in new passenger vehicles through tax credits and standards	1.6	4.9
Accelerate oil savings in motor vehicles through		
fuel efficient replacement tires and motor oil	0.5	0.6
efficiency improvements in heavy-duty trucks	0.5	1.1
Accelerate oil savings in industrial, aviation, and residential sectors	0.3	0.7
Encourage growth of biofuels industry through demonstration and standards	0.3	3.9
Total oil saved	3.2	11.2

TAKEN FROM: David C. Hawkins "Testimony of... Before Full Committee Hearing on Coal Liquefaction and Gasification," [Committee on Energy and Natural Resources, U.S. Senate] April 24, 2006.

plants are not inherently "clean." If such plants are to operate with minimum emissions of conventional pollutants, performance standards will need to be written—standards that do not exist today in the U.S. as far as we are aware. In addition, the various federal emission cap programs now in force would apply to few, if any, coal-to-liquids plants.

Thus, we cannot say today that coal-to-liquids plants will be required to meet stringent emission performance standards adequate to prevent either significant localized impacts or regional emissions impacts. . . .

Water Pollution

Coal production causes negative physical and chemical changes to nearby waters. In all surface mining, the overburden (earth layers above the coal seams) is removed and deposited on the surface as waste rock. The most significant physical effect on water occurs from valley fills, the waste rock associated with mountaintop removal (MTR) mining. Since MTR mining started in the United States in the early '70s, studies estimate that over 700 miles of streams have been buried from valley fills, and 1200 additional miles have been directly impacted from valley fills through sedimentation or chemistry alteration. Together, the waterways harmed by valley fills are about 80 percent as long as the Mississippi River. Valley fills bury the headwaters of streams, which in the southeastern U.S. support diverse and unique habitats, and regulate nutrients, water quality, and flow quantity. The elimination of headwaters therefore has long-reaching impacts many miles downstream.

Coal mining can also lead to increased sedimentation, which affects both water chemistry and stream flow, and negatively impacts aquatic habitat. Valley fills in the eastern U.S., as well as waste rock from strip mines in the West add sediment to streams, as does the construction and use of roads in the mining complex. A final physical impact of mining on water is to the hydrology of aquifers. MTR and valley fills remove upper drainage basins, and often connect two previously separate aquifers, altering the surrounding groundwater recharge scheme.

Acid mine drainage (AMD) is the most significant form of chemical pollution produced from coal mining operations. In both underground and surface mining, sulfur-bearing minerals common in coal mining areas are brought up to the surface in waste rock. When these minerals come in contact with precipitation and groundwater, an acidic leachate is formed. This leachate picks up heavy metals and carries these toxins into streams or groundwater. Waters affected by AMD often exhibit increased levels of sulfate, total dissolved solids, calcium, selenium, magnesium, manganese, conductivity, acidity, sodium, nitrate, and nitrite. This drastically changes stream and groundwater chemistry. The degraded water becomes less habitable, non-potable, and unfit for recreational purposes.

The acidity and metals can also corrode structures such as culverts and bridges. In the eastern U.S., estimates of the damage from AMD range from four to eleven thousand miles of streams. In the West, estimates are between five and ten thousand miles of streams polluted. The effects of AMD can be diminished through addition of alkaline substances to counteract the acid, but recent studies have found that the addition of alkaline material can increase the mobilization of both selenium and arsenic. AMD is costly to mitigate, requiring over $40 million annually in Kentucky, Tennessee, Virginia, and West Virginia alone.

Air Pollution

There are two main sources of air pollution during the coal production process. The first is methane emissions from the mines. Methane is a powerful heat-trapping gas and is the second most important contributor to global warming after carbon dioxide. Methane emissions from coal mines make up between 10 and 15% of anthropogenic methane emissions in the U.S. According to the most recent official inventory of U.S. global warming emissions, coal mining results in the release of 3 million tons of methane per year, which is equivalent to 68 million tons of carbon dioxide.

The second significant form of air pollution from coal mining is particulate matter (PM) emissions. While methane emissions are largely due to eastern underground mines, PM emissions are particularly serious at western surface mines. The arid, open and frequently windy region allows for the creation and transport of significant amounts of particulate matter in connection with mining operations. Fugitive dust emissions occur during nearly every phase of coal strip mining in the West. The most significant sources of these emissions are removal of the overburden through blasting and use of draglines, truck haulage of the overburden and mined coal, road grading, and wind erosion of reclaimed areas. PM emissions from diesel trucks and equipment used in mining are also significant. PM can cause serious respiratory damage as well as premature death. In 2002, one of Wyoming's coal-producing counties, Campbell County, exceeded its ambient air quality threshold several times, almost earning non-attainment status. Coal dust problems in the West are likely to get worse if the administration finalizes its January 2006 proposal to exempt mining (and other activities) from controls aimed at meeting the coarse PM standard.

Coal Mine Wastes

Coal mining leaves a legacy of wastes long after mining operations cease. One significant waste is the sludge that is produced from washing coal. There are currently over 700 sludge impoundments located throughout mining regions, and this number continues to grow. These impoundment ponds pose a potential threat to the environment and human life. If an impoundment fails, the result can be disastrous. In 1972 an impoundment break in West Virginia released a flood of coal sludge that killed 125 people. In the year 2000 an impoundment break in Kentucky involving more than 300 million gallons of slurry (30 times the size of the *Exxon Valdez* spill) killed all aquatic life in a 20-mile diameter, destroyed homes, and contaminated much of the drinking water in the eastern part of the state.

Another waste from coal mining is the solid waste rock left behind from tunneling or blasting. This can result in a number of environmental impacts previously discussed, including acid mine drainage (AMD). A common problem with coal mine legacies is the fact that if a mine is abandoned or a mining company goes out of business, the former owner is under no legal obligation to clean up and monitor the environmental wastes, leaving the responsibility in the hands of the state.

A Responsible Action Plan

The impacts that a large coal-to-liquids program could have on global warming pollution, conventional air pollution and damage from expanded coal production are substantial. Before deciding whether to invest scores, perhaps hundreds of billions of dollars in a new industry like coal-to-liquids, we need a much more serious assessment of whether this is an industry that should proceed at all.

Fortunately, the U.S. can have a robust and effective program to reduce oil dependence without rushing into an embrace of coal-to-liquids technologies. A combination of efficiency, renewable fuels and ... plug-in hybrid vehicles can reduce our oil consumption more quickly, more cleanly and in larger amounts than coal-to-liquids even on the massive scale advocated by Peabody Energy.

A combination of more efficient cars, trucks and planes, biofuels, and "smart growth" transportation options outlined in the report "Securing America," produced by NRDC and the Institute for the Analysis of Global Security, can cut oil dependence by more than 3 million barrels a day in 10 years, and achieve cuts of more than 11 million barrels a day by 2025, far outstripping the 2.6 million barrel a day program being promoted by Peabody. . . .

To cut our dependence on oil we should follow a simple rule: start with the measures that will produce the quickest, cleanest and least expensive reductions in oil use; measures that will put us on track to achieve the reductions in global warming emissions we need to protect the climate. If we are thoughtful about the actions we take, our country can pursue an energy path that enhances our security, our economy, and our environment.

Periodical and Internet Sources Bibliography

The following articles have been selected to supplement the diverse views presented in this chapter.

American Association for the Advancement of Science	"Coal-to-Liquid Technology," *AAAS Policy Brief*, April 10, 2009.
H. Sterling Burnett	"Don't Let Deepwater Deep-Six Offshore Drilling," National Center for Policy Analysis, May 3, 2010. www.ncpa.org.
Denver Post	"Cap and Trade Is Wrong Solution," June 26, 2009.
Robert H. Frank	"Of Individual Liberty and Cap and Trade," *New York Times*, January 9, 2010.
James Hansen	"Cap and Fade," *New York Times*, December 6, 2009.
Kevin Hassett	"Big Spill's Bad Timing Puts Oil Drilling at Risk," Bloomberg.com, September 14, 2009. www.bloomberg.com.
Steven F. Hayward and Kenneth P. Green	"Waxman-Markey: An Exercise in Unreality," *Energy and Environmental Outlook*, July 2009.
Paul Krugman	"Building a Green Economy," *New York Times*, April 7, 2010.
Robert J. Michaels	"Renewables Aren't the Answer," *USA Today*, October 20, 2008.
Wall Street Journal	"Who Pays for Cap and Trade?" March 9, 2009.

For Further Discussion

Chapter 1

1. The American Lung Association contends that air pollution continues to be a serious problem, requiring stricter standards. Joel Schwartz counters that although energy use is increasing, air pollution continues to decrease; thus stricter standards are unnecessary. Identify the evidence the authors use to support their claims. Which evidence do you find more persuasive? Explain.

2. Kurt Marko argues that electronic waste poses a more challenging problem than municipal waste, thus requiring efforts to make disposal safer over the full life cycle of e-products. Do you think Beverly Thorpe's producer responsibility recommendations will address Marko's concerns? Why or why not?

3. Richard Grant and Carl Bialik agree that the size and impact of the plastic gyre in the Pacific Ocean is unknown, yet Grant believes the problem is a serious one while Bialik claims the problem may be exaggerated. These authors use very different rhetorical techniques to support their position on this issue. Which argument do you find more persuasive?

4. Of the pollution threats explored in this chapter, which do you think is the most serious? Explain.

Chapter 2

1. What commonalities can you find in the rhetoric used by the authors on both sides of the debate over what technologies will best reduce pollution? Which arguments do you find most persuasive? Explain.

2. Robert S. Giglio and Jeff Biggers contest whether clean coal technology will reduce air pollution. How do the affiliations of the authors of these two viewpoints influence their arguments? Does this influence make their arguments more or less persuasive? Explain.

3. Siena Kaplan, Brad Heavner, and Rob Sargent argue that plug-in cars will help reduce air pollution while James R. Healey argues that plug-in cars will increase pollution. All agree that some electricity sources are not clean. Do you think that the investment in clean energy that Kaplan, Heavner, and Sargent recommend is sufficient to allay Healey's concerns?

4. Do you agree with the World Policy Institute that growing energy needs require a reasoned approach in which some pollution risks are acceptable? Do any of the arguments against ethanol made by Sasha Lilley influence your answer? Why or why not?

5. The Nuclear Energy Institute argues that nuclear power should be part of any emission reduction program. Travis Madsen, Tony Dutzik, Bernadette Del Chiaro, and Rob Sargent claim, however, that nuclear power will hinder plants to reduce pollution. Which argument do you find more persuasive? Explain.

Chapter 3

1. Of the ways in which communities might reduce pollution that are explored in this chapter, which do you think is the best alternative? Explain.

2. Robert H. Frank claims that buying carbon offsets will help reduce the human carbon footprint. Doug Struck believes that carbon-offset programs are easily abused. Frank and Struck appear to have different views on human nature. Identify these differing views. With which view of human nature do you agree and why?

Chapter 4

1. What commonalities can you find in the rhetoric used by the authors on both sides of the debate over what federal pollution-reduction policies are best? Which rhetorical strategies do you find most persuasive? Explain.

2. How do the affiliations of the authors in this chapter influence their arguments? Does this influence make their arguments more or less persuasive? Explain, citing from the viewpoints.

3. John Podesta and Kenneth Green dispute whether cap-and-trade policies will promote or limit pollution-reduction innovation. Which viewpoint do you find more persuasive? Explain.

4. Of the federal pollution-reduction policies discussed in this chapter, which do you believe will best reduce pollution? Explain your answer.

Organizations to Contact

The editors have compiled the following list of organizations concerned with the issues debated in this book. The descriptions are derived from materials provided by the organizations. All have publications or information available for interested readers. The list was compiled on the date of publication of the present volume; the information provided here may change. Be aware that many organizations take several weeks or longer to respond to inquiries, so allow as much time as possible.

American Council for an Energy-Efficient Economy (ACEEE)
529 Fourteenth Street NW, Suite 600
Washington, DC   20045-1000
(202) 507-4000 • fax: (202) 429-2248
website: www.aceee.org

The American Council for an Energy-Efficient Economy (ACEEE) supports energy-efficiency measures to promote economic prosperity and environmental protection. It conducts policy analyses, advises policy makers, and educates businesses and consumers through reports, books, conference proceedings, and media outreach. On its website, ACEEE publishes fact sheets and reports, including "Plug-In Electric Vehicles: Penetration and Grid Impacts" and *States Stepping Forward: Best Practices for State-Led Energy Efficiency Programs.*

American Council on Science and Health (ACSH)
1995 Broadway, 2nd Floor, New York, NY   10023-5860
(212) 362-7044 • fax: (212) 362-4919
e-mail: acsh@acsh.org
website: www.acsh.org

The American Council on Science and Health (ACSH) is a consumer education consortium concerned with, among other topics, issues related to the environment and health. The council publishes editorials, position papers, and books, including "No Oil Spills with the Nuclear Option" and "The Deadly War Against DDT," which are available on its website.

American Lung Association (ALA)
1301 Pennsylvania Avenue NW, Suite 800
Washington, DC   20004
(202) 785-3355 • fax: (202) 452-1805
e-mail: info@lungusa.org
website: www.lungusa.org

Founded in 1904 to fight tuberculosis, the American Lung Association (ALA) currently fights lung disease in all its forms, with special emphasis on asthma, tobacco control, and environmental health. Under the Air Quality link on its website, the ALA provides articles, fact sheets, and special reports on pollution-related issues, including its yearly "State of the Air."

Cato Institute
1000 Massachusetts Avenue NW
Washington, DC   20001-5403
(202) 842-0200 • fax: (202) 842-3490
e-mail: cato@cato.org
website: www.cato.org

The Cato Institute is a libertarian public policy research foundation dedicated to limiting the role of government and protecting individual liberties. The institute publishes the quarterly magazine *Regulation* and the bimonthly *Cato Policy Report*. It disapproves of Environmental Protection Agency (EPA) regulations, considering them too stringent. On its website, the institute publishes many of its papers dealing with the environment, including "High-Speed Rail: The Wrong Road for America," "Plug-In Pablum," and "The Gulf Spill and Compensation for Disaster Victims."

Clean Air-Cool Planet
100 Market Street, Suite 204, Portsmouth, NH   03801
(603) 422-6464 • fax: (603) 422-6441

e-mail: info@cleanair-coolplanet.org
website: www.cleanair-coolplanet.org

Clean Air-Cool Planet partners with businesses, colleges, and communities in the Northeast to reduce carbon emissions and educate the public and opinion leaders about global warming impacts and solutions. The organization publishes fact sheets and reports, including "Climate Change and Arctic Wildlife" and *Getting to Zero: Defining Corporate Carbon Neutrality*, which are available on its website.

Clear Air Markets Program

US Environmental Protection Agency
1200 Pennsylvania Avenue NW, Mail Code 6204J
Washington, DC   20460
(202) 343-9150
website: www.epa.gov/airmarkets

The Clear Air Markets Program of the Environmental Protection Agency administers market-based programs to reduce emissions. The program is based on the belief that market-based emission-reduction programs will best improve human health and the natural environment. The program's goal is to lower outdoor concentrations of fine particles, ozone, mercury, and other significant air emissions. Its website provides information on cap and trade, allowance trading, and emissions monitoring as well as the effects of acid rain, smog, mercury, and climate change.

Coal River Mountain Watch

PO Box 651, Whitesville, WV   25209
(304) 854-2182
website: www.crmw.net

The Coal River Mountain Watch is a local grassroots organization that works to halt mountaintop mining in West Virginia. It was founded in response to the fear and frustration of those living near or downstream from huge mountaintop removal sites. Volunteers organize the residents of southern

West Virginia to fight for social, economic, and environmental justice. The organization publishes the *Coal River Mountain Watch Messenger*, recent issues of which are available on its website.

Coal-to-Liquids Coalition

(202) 463-2644

website: www.futurecoalfuels.org

The Coal-to-Liquids Coalition, which is made up of labor, mining, and industry groups, promotes liquefied-coal fuels to help secure American energy supplies. The coalition believes that because the United States has abundant and affordable coal reserves, proven gasification and liquefaction technologies can help reduce the nation's increasing dependence on foreign energy supplies and serve as a source of transportation fuel while protecting the environment. Fact sheets on the security, economic, and environment benefits of liquid coal technologies and recent issues of its newsletter, *FutureCoalFuels.org Update*, are available on its website.

Competitive Enterprise Institute (CEI)

1899 L Street NW, 12th Floor, Washington, DC   20036

(202) 331-1010 • fax: (202) 331-0640

e-mail: info@cei.org

website: www.cei.org

The Competitive Enterprise Institute (CEI) is a public policy organization dedicated to the principles of free enterprise and limited government. The institute believes that consumers are best helped not by government regulation but by being allowed to make their own choices in a free marketplace and thus supports market-based pollution policies. On its website, CEI publishes articles, editorials, speeches, and studies, including "Asthma Cap-and-Trade Schemes Are Not Markets," "No More Ethanol for America, Please," and "Big Green Regulations Suffocate Jobs, Economic Growth?"

Earth Island Institute
2150 Allston Way, Suite 460, Berkeley, CA 94704-1375
(510) 859-9100 • fax: (510) 859-9091
website: www.earthisland.org

Founded in 1982 by veteran environmentalist David Brower, Earth Island Institute develops and supports projects that counteract threats to the biological and cultural diversity that sustain the environment. Through education and activism, Earth Island promotes the conservation, preservation, and restoration of the earth. It publishes the quarterly *Earth Island Journal*. Recent articles are available on the institute's website, including "We Are All Louisianans," "Plastic Pollution Coalition: The Bioplastic Labyrinth," and "Plastic Island 'Ecocide': The Filth War Crime?"

Energy Information Administration (EIA)
1000 Independence Avenue SW, Washington, DC 20585
(202) 586-8800
website: www.eia.doe.gov

The central source for US government data and forecasts on energy, the Energy Information Administration (EIA), an agency within the US Department of Energy, collects, analyzes, and disseminates energy information to promote sound policy making, efficient markets, and public understanding of energy and its interaction with the economy and the environment. On its website, the EIA publishes fact sheets, data, reports, and analyses on energy sources including coal, nuclear, and biofuels.

Environmental Protection Agency (EPA)
Ariel Rios Building, 1200 Pennsylvania Avenue NW
Washington, DC 20460
(202) 272-0167
website: www.epa.gov

The Environmental Protection Agency (EPA) is the US federal agency in charge of protecting the environment and controlling pollution. The agency works toward these goals by assisting businesses and local environmental agencies, enacting and enforcing regulations, identifying and fining polluters, and cleaning up polluted sites. On its website, EPA has links to specific pollution issues under its main links: Water, Air, Climate, Wastes and Pollution, Green Living, Human Health, and Ecosystems. These links include articles, memos, and speeches on a wide variety of pollution-related topics.

Friends of the Earth
1100 Fifteenth Street NW, 11th Floor, Washington, DC   20005
(202) 783-7400 • fax: (202) 783-0444
e-mail: foe@foe.org
website: www.foe.org

Friends of the Earth is a national advocacy organization dedicated to protecting the planet from environmental degradation; preserving biological, cultural, and ethnic diversity; and empowering citizens to have an influential voice in decisions affecting the quality of their environment. It publishes the quarterly *Friends of the Earth Newsmagazine*, recent and archived issues of which are available on its website.

Heritage Foundation
214 Massachusetts Avenue NE, Washington, DC   20002-4999
(202) 546-4400 • fax: (202) 544-6979
e-mail: info@heritage.org
website: www.heritage.org

The Heritage Foundation is a conservative think tank that supports free enterprise and limited government. Its researchers criticize Environmental Protection Agency (EPA) overregulation and believe that recycling is an ineffective method of dealing with waste. Its publications, such as the quarterly *Policy Review*, include studies on the uncertainty of global warming and the greenhouse effect. The articles "The Costs of Cap and Trade," "Green Protectionism," and "The Economic Impact of an Offshore Drilling Ban" are available on its website.

Lifestyles of Health and Sustainability (LOHAS)

833 West South Boulder Road, Louisville, CO   80027
(303) 222-8263
website: www.lohas.com

Lifestyles of Health and Sustainability (LOHAS) sponsors an annual business conference focused on the marketplace for goods and services related to health, the environment, social justice, personal development, and sustainable living. It also publishes a weekly online newsletter and the annual *LOHAS Journal*. On its website, LOHAS provides access to recent articles from its publications, including "Understanding the LOHAS Consumer: The Rise of Ethical Consumerism" and "Following the Waste Stream." LOHAS also publishes a business directory and resources based on each LOHAS category.

Natural Resources Defense Council (NRDC)

40 W. Twentieth Street, New York, NY   10011
(212) 727-2700
e-mail: proinfo@nrdc.org
website: www.nrdc.org

The Natural Resources Defense Council (NRDC) is a non-profit organization that uses law, science, and more than four hundred thousand members nationwide to protect the planet's wildlife and wild places and to ensure a safe and healthy environment for all living things. On its website, NRDC provides links to specific pollution-related topics such as Clean Air and Energy, Global Warming, Clean Water and Oceans, and Toxic Chemicals and Health. These links include fact sheets, reports, and articles, such as "The Campaign to Dump Dirty Diesel," "Pollution from Giant Livestock Farms Threatens Public Health," and "Pesticides Threaten Farm Children's Health."

Office of Surface Mining Reclamation and Enforcement (OSM)

1951 Constitution Avenue NW, Washington, DC   20240
(202) 208-2719

e-mail: GetInfo@osmre.gov
website: www.osmre.gov

Office of Surface Mining Reclamation and Enforcement (OSM) is a bureau within the US Department of the Interior that is responsible for establishing a nationwide program to protect society and the environment from the adverse effects of surface coal mining operations. Because today most coal states have developed their own programs, OSM works with colleges, universities, and other state and federal agencies to further the science of reclaiming mined lands and protecting the environment through such initiatives as planting more trees and establishing much-needed wildlife habitats. Reports, statistics, and links to OSM directives, guidelines, and mining laws and regulations are available on its website.

Physicians for Social Responsibility (PSR)

1875 Connecticut Avenue NW, Suite 1012
Washington, DC   20009
(202) 667-4260 • fax: (202) 667-4201
e-mail: psrnatl@psr.org
website: www.psr.org

Founded in 1961, Physicians for Social Responsibility (PSR) documented the presence of strontium-90—a highly radioactive waste product of atmospheric nuclear testing—in American children's teeth. This finding led rapidly to the Limited Test Ban Treaty that ended aboveground nuclear explosions by the superpowers. PSR's mission is to address public health threats that affect people in the United States and around the world. PSR's website publishes fact sheets and article excerpts, including "Coal Ash: The Toxic Threat to Our Health and Environment" and "Is There a Nuclear Revival in the United States?"

Property and Environment Research Center (PERC)

2048 Analysis Drive, Suite A, Bozeman, MT   59718
(406) 587-9591 • fax: (406) 586-7555

e-mail: perc@perc.org
website: www.perc.org

The Property and Environment Research Center (PERC) is a nonprofit research and educational organization that seeks market-oriented solutions to environmental problems. Areas of research covered in the PERC Policy Series papers include endangered species, forestry, fisheries, mines, parks, public lands, property rights, hazardous waste, pollution, water, and wildlife. PERC conducts a variety of conferences, offers internships and fellowships, and provides environmental education materials. On its website, PERC provides access to recent and archived articles, reports, and its policy series, including "Not the Time to Cap and Trade" and "The Waste of Recycling."

Worldwatch Institute

1776 Massachusetts Avenue NW
Washington, DC   20036-1904
(202) 452-1999 • fax: (202) 296-7365
e-mail: worldwatch@worldwatch.org
website: www.worldwatch.org

The Worldwatch Institute is a nonprofit public policy research organization dedicated to informing policy makers and the public about emerging global problems and trends and the complex links between the world economy and its environmental support systems. The institute publishes the bimonthly *World Watch* magazine, the Environmental Alert series, and several policy papers. Recent and archived issues of *World Watch* are available on its website.

Bibliography of Books

Carolyn Abbot   *Enforcing Pollution Control Regulation: Strengthening Sanctions and Improving Deterrence.* Portland, OR: Hart Pub., 2009.

Robert U. Ayres and Edward H. Ayres   *Crossing the Energy Divide: Moving from Fossil Fuel Dependence to a Clean-Energy Future.* Upper Saddle River, NJ: Wharton School Pub., 2010.

Peter Barnes   *Climate Solutions: A Citizen's Guide.* White River Junction, VT: Chelsea Green Publishing, 2008.

James T. Bartis, Frank Camm, and David S. Ortiz   *Producing Liquid Fuels from Coal: Prospects and Policy Issues.* Santa Monica, CA: RAND Corporation, 2008.

Todd P. Carington, ed.   *Carbon Capture and Storage Including Coal-Fired Power Plants.* New York: Nova Science Publishers, 2010.

Robert W. Collin   *The Environmental Protection Agency: Cleaning Up America's Act.* Westport, CT: Greenwood Press, 2006.

Daniel C. Esty and Andrew S. Winston   *Green to Gold: How Smart Companies Use Environmental Strategy to Innovate, Create Value, and Build Competitive Advantage.* Hoboken, NJ: Wiley, 2009.

Jody Freeman and Charles D. Kolstad, eds.
Moving to Markets in Environmental Regulation: Lessons from Twenty Years of Experience. New York: Oxford University Press, 2007.

Allen Fuhs
Hybrid Vehicles and the Future of Personal Transportation. Boca Raton, FL: CRC Press, 2009.

Peter C. Fusaro and Marion Yuen
Green Trading Markets: Developing the Second Wave. Boston: Elsevier, 2005.

George A. Gonzalez
The Politics of Air Pollution: Urban Growth, Ecological Modernization, and Symbolic Inclusion. Albany: State University of New York Press, 2005.

Jeff Goodell
Big Coal: The Dirty Secret Behind America's Energy Future. Boston: Houghton Mifflin, 2007.

Elizabeth Grossman
High Tech Trash: Digital Devices, Hidden Toxics, and Human Health. Washington, DC: Island Press, 2006.

Ram B. Gupta and Ayhan Demirbas
Gasoline, Diesel, and Ethanol Biofuels from Grasses and Plants. New York: Cambridge University Press, 2010.

David W. Hafemeister
Physics of Societal Issues: Calculations on National Security, Environment, and Energy. New York: Springer, 2007.

Jeff Hay, ed.
Issues on Trial: Pollution. Farmington Hills, MI: Greenhaven Press, 2009.

Kathryn Hilgenkamp	*Environmental Health: Ecological Perspectives.* Sudbury, MA: Jones and Bartlett, 2005.
Edward Humes	*Eco Barons: The Dreamers, Schemers, and Millionaires Who Are Saving Our Planet.* New York: Ecco, 2009.
Thomas M. Kostigen	*You Are Here: Exposing the Vital Link Between What We Do and What That Does to Our Planet.* New York: HarperOne, 2008.
Oliver G. Krenshaw, ed.	*Cruise Ship Pollution.* New York: Nova Science, 2009.
Klaus Kümmerer	*Pharmaceuticals in the Environment: Sources, Fate, Effects and Risks.* 3rd ed. New York: Springer, 2008.
David M. Mousdale	*Biofuels: Biotechnology, Chemistry, and Sustainable Development.* Boca Raton, FL: CRC Press, 2008.
National Research Council	*Coal: Research and Development to Support National Energy Policy.* Washington, DC: National Academies Press, 2007.
David Pimentel, ed.	*Biofuels, Solar and Wind as Renewable Energy Systems: Benefits and Risks.* New York: Springer, 2008.
Heather Rogers	*Green Gone Wrong: How Our Economy Is Undermining the Environmental Revolution.* New York: Scribner, 2010.

Walter A. Rosenbaum — *Environmental Politics and Policy*. 8th ed. Washington, DC: CQ Press, 2008.

David B. Sandalow, ed. — *Plug-in Electric Vehicles: What Role for Washington?* Washington, DC: Brookings Institution Press, 2009.

Giles Slade — *Made to Break: Technology and Obsolescence in America*. Cambridge, MA: Harvard University Press, 2006.

Ted Smith, David A. Sonnenfeld, and David Naguib Pellow, eds. — *Challenging the Chip: Labor Rights and Environmental Justice in the Global Electronics Industry*. Philadelphia, PA: Temple University Press, 2006.

Daniel Sperling and James S. Cannon, eds. — *Driving Climate Change: Cutting Carbon from Transportation*. Boston: Elsevier, 2007.

Patrick J. Sullivan, Franklin J. Agardy, and James J.J. Clark — *The Environmental Science of Drinking Water*. Burlington, MA: Elsevier Butterworth-Heinemann, 2005.

Andrew Szasz — *Shopping Our Way to Safety: How We Changed from Protecting the Environment to Protecting Ourselves*. Minneapolis: University of Minnesota Press, 2007.

Daniel A. Vallero — *Fundamentals of Air Pollution*. Boston: Elsevier, 2008.

John Wargo — *Green Intelligence: Creating Environments That Protect Human Health*. New Haven, CT: Yale University Press, 2009.

Index